FURTHER CASE STUDIES IN HOTEL MANAGEMENT

FURTHER CASE STUDIES IN HOTEL MANAGEMENT

GAYNOR HOTEL CO. LTD.

By

Roger Doswell

and

Philip Nailon

Reader in Management Studies
University of Surrey

With a foreword by John Fuller, Quondam Professor of
Hotel Management and Director, Scottish Hotel School,
University of Strathclyde, Glasgow

To Malcolm Baldwin

with all best wishes

from Philip Nailon

October 1977

BARRIE & JENKINS

COMMUNICA - EUROPA

First published in 1977 by
Barrie & Jenkins Ltd
24 Highbury Crescent, London, N5 1RX

ISBN 0 214 20342 5

Printed in Great Britain at the Alden Press, Oxford

We dedicate this book to
our respective wives
Mary and Harriett

CONTENTS

FOREWORD

By John Fuller

Way back in 1967 I welcomed in a foreword the appearance of this book's forerunner, *Case Studies in Hotel Management* by Roger Doswell and Philip Nailon. That first book was timely not only because of its intrinsic merits but because of the dearth then of management literature applied to our industry in general and of hotel management case studies in particular. That Doswell and Nailon's first book met a need is evidenced by its resulting in a third edition and being still in print and in demand today.

What is remarkable is that ten years later there continues to be a shortage of published case study material for teachers, students and practitioners of hotel management. Thus this Doswell and Nailon sequel, *Further Case Studies*, is just as timely as its predecessor. I am confident that both books will be in demand for many a year to come.

Further Case Studies is very much in the style, and with the approach, of its predecessor but opens new spheres for study. It is thus complementary to, and in no way a substitute for, the earlier volume.

Deceptively easy to read, Doswell and Nailon's exposé of both philosophical and practical considerations of management in the hotel field is calculated not only to support teachers and students but to make managers themselves think afresh about their task. Their existing case studies have already proved to be valuable aids in the classroom situation; so will their new ones. I believe this new book will also help managers themselves to re-appraise their task, to be stimulated in performing it and to find fresh satisfaction in their calling.

Adderbury, Oxford
January 1977

INTRODUCTION

'Painters and poets,' you say, 'have always had a bold license for bold invention.' We know this; we claim the liberty for ourselves and we give it to others.

HORACE

In our previous book, *Case Studies in Hotel Management*, the chief characters were Charles Gaynor and Adam Smith. In this book we have continued to portray them in their respective roles as the Managing Director and his personal assistant of the fictitious Gaynor Hotel Co. Ltd. Gaynor is a man in his fifties, sallow and grey haired, who inherited the Company, which now consists of ten hotels, from his father. Adam studied hotel management for four years at a college in England before working for a year in a Gaynor Hotel, the Parthenon. He decided to go to the United States of America where he obtained a graduate degree in business administration at a Middle Western University. On returning to England he became assistant to the General Manager of the Delphi, another Gaynor Hotel, until he was appointed special investigations assistant to Gaynor eighteen months later.

The purpose of this book is the same as *Case Studies*: to involve the reader in events and issues in the life of a fictitious hotel company. We have attempted again to evoke the reality of management activity and the ambiguity, conflict and equivocation experienced in a business setting.

Since *Case Studies* was published we have received many comments from people at all levels of management, and even different cultures, about the portrayed events in the Gaynor Hotel Co. We have been gratified and grateful for these comments; a frequent comment has been that we have written about events personally experienced by other people. We feel that this indicates a range of common experiences in the fascinating world of hotel operation and are encouraged to offer another book about Gaynor Hotels in the hope that our synthesis may be of interest and, possibly, of help.

The authors are still convinced that the best way to develop greater knowledge, insights and skills in the practice of management is by an examination of the actuality of day to day management of operations. A dearth of systematic knowledge exists about what hotel managers actually do, but from our experience have tried to create events which demonstrate what must be done and how the manager must react and respond.

Complaints are frequently voiced about the inability of graduates from our hotel schools to apply their theoretical knowledge, or that this knowledge is irrelevant to the real world of business. The graduate might justifiably respond by saying that it is not possible to create pressures for business survival and success in the classroom. But he has had experience of pressures, such as those created by our examination system—and survived. Limitations of time and other resources often force the management teacher into adopting a normative approach, that is 'the way things *should* be done'. The basis of this is often doubtful and frequently derived from a mythology of a bygone era; the essentially pragmatic approach of hotel management, needs to be based on concepts derived from a descriptive approach realistically associated with 'the way things are'.

The graduate who has developed a frozen normative mentality is stunned by confrontation with reality on entering industry. Perhaps the impossible standards acquired create a disillusionment and, for the sake of a quiet life, he quickly conforms to the standards which he finds. Whatever fire may have existed is extinguished and he sides with those who disdain the 'theoretical' without distinguishing between good and bad theory.

But it is not only the graduating student who experiences frustration and conformity; the practising manager moving through the constant kaleidoscope of events which typify hotel life, seldom seems to have the opportunity to reflect on his experience and teaze out the concepts involved. The hotel manager, like a captain on a ship, frequently experiences some isolation because he is limited in the range of people with whom he can share ideas, fears and feelings of insecurity without losing status.

Neither of these problems will be solved by reading a book but we hope that by making some effort to identify with the characters of *this* book some inspiration may be found. In this way we hope that answers may be found to the questions, 'Do I agree, and why?' or 'I don't agree, and why?' Again we ask our readers not just to read, but also to *experience* each of the situations as they occur.

For the most part we have continued to represent events by the use of question and answer in the Socratic manner. In this way we hope to demonstrate the flavour of management activity as an ambiguous process rarely resulting in 'right' or 'wrong' answers. The

INTRODUCTION 13

characters and situations have therefore been created as a vehicle for our purpose and do not, intentionally, represent anybody living or dead. We must also emphasis that the opinions expressed by the characters are their own and not necessarily those of the authors.

We regard this book as a continuation of *Case Studies in Hotel Management*, and have therefore indicated by footnotes (CS) relevant topics appearing in that earlier work.

Finally, we are indebted to the many people who, in each of our careers, have helped us to learn. We are equally indebted to those people who, by their management malpractices, have made us angry and provoked our thinking. Finally, we are also indebted to those many people who have taken 'old' Charles Gaynor and 'young' Adam Smith into their lives.

1

WHAT IS MANAGEMENT?

*A thing may look specious in theory, and yet be
ruinous in practice; a thing may look evil in theory,
and yet be in practice excellent.*

EDMUND BURKE

Adam Smith sat at his desk and reflected that it was now exactly
twelve months since he had been appointed general assistant to
Charles Gaynor, Managing Director of Gaynor Hotels. During this
time he had been used as adviser, counsellor, internal consultant and
therapist. He had investigated problems, developed concepts,
established principles and generally contributed to the decision
taking process which took place in the mind of his employer,
Gaynor.

His attention had been attracted by an article he had been
reading, which said:

In order to maintain its internal dynamic which is essential to
progress, a company needs the existence of a rebel group which is
primarily concerned with challenging company policy; a group
which regards as its main function the generation of sceptical
attitudes towards the company's methods of operation, organization and policies. Such a group should adopt as a working
principle the slogan, 'if it works it's obsolescent'. In other words
the mere fact that a system is working satisfactorily should in itself
be sufficient reason for its re-examination.[1]

Adam ruminated on this and considered that with Carson, his
assistant, they really had created a two-man management services
activity since they had concentrated on looking at, and solving, old
problems in new ways. A pocket of rational thought in a wilderness
of emotionalism—if only that were really true, thought Adam!

He felt depressed, although he realised that some progress had
been made, it seemed infinitesimal when one looked at the company
as a whole. Where is the real answer to the achievement of progress,
thought Adam, if only one could put one's finger on it. Particular
aspects, methods, solutions and so on were looked at which all

[1] Ward, T. R., Management Services—The Way Ahead, *National O & M
Conference*, 1964; published as an **Anbar Monograph**, Anbar Publications, 1965

seemed part of the answer, but where was the whole answer? Charles Gaynor, although a man inculcated at an early age with the attitudes and ways of traditional hotelkeeping, was most receptive to new ideas; indeed, he could generate them himself and boasted of his preparedness to accept necessary change. But nothing much seemed to have changed in these twelve months; Gaynor Hotels was still making a profit, its managers were still 'managing' but problems continued to abound and there seemed just as many unanswered questions.

Adam leaned forward on his desk with his head in his hands, he wondered if the company was really progressing, if things were any better, and whether he was just deceiving himself. Perhaps the problem was that the company was just 'managing', that it was just getting by, just keeping its head above water. Is it really geared to grow and develop and prosper, is it really looking ahead and ready to exploit the changing circumstances of a changing world? That's the central question, thought Adam, and I wish I could answer it confidently.

Management! It is all in the management, a handful of men cannot carry a company—it is in the strength and depth of *all* the people who form the firm. His thoughts were interrupted by the door opening and Gaynor appearing with a benevolent smile, and a friendly 'Good afternoon, Adam.'

Gaynor: I thought I would let you know it looks as though I will have to fire a manager, or to put it euphemistically, to ask him to resign.

Adam: Who is it, sir?

Gaynor: Hedges, at the Zephyr. Nasty business and the sort of scandal I deplore. I had a letter from a Mr. Coloniki; his wife is secretary to Hedges who, he asserted, has been sleeping with her. I thought there couldn't be anything in it and I referred it to our Mr. Hedges never expecting anything other than a denial. Well the damn fool confirmed it as being true, he *has* been sleeping with his secretary. Doesn't leave me much alternative, does it? I can't compromise my principles and I will not have my hotel executives entering into this sort of relationship with their staff. My goodness! What sort of an example is it? Oh, the stupid man, and he was doing quite a good job for us.

Adam: Well, sir, there's an old Hungarian proverb which say that when a man's fancy is titillated his brain goes to water.

Gaynor: How very true! But a little control, a little sense of responsibility, a little maturity, that's all I ask. It isn't even as if he was serious about her; as he told me, it was just his 'little indiscretion' and he hoped that I wouldn't find out. By the way, you didn't already know about it, did you?

Adam: No, certainly not, sir. I haven't heard the slightest suggestion.

Gaynor: Well, back to the old problem of finding a new manager; as if good managers grew on trees! They are such rare animals, they take such a great deal of finding, such a great deal of raising.

Adam: How about his assistant, Gripple, do you think that he might be ready to take over?

Gaynor: He might. ... I don't know, even if we knew what job we were really picking him for; I mean, what *is* management, what is it *really*? What are we looking for?

Adam: Well, quite honestly, sir, I do not think that he's ready. I think he could develop into a manager, but he needs more time.

Gaynor: All right, we will have to find somebody. I'll tell you what we can do: you take over as manager of the Zephyr for the next month or so. During that time I will find a new manager. This *has* caught us unawares, I can't think of anybody suitable in the company at present.

Adam: But I've never actually managed an hotel!

Gaynor: Well, it will be an excellent experience for you. Anyway, I have no doubt about *your* management abilities. But you still didn't answer my question just now. What actually *is* management—do you know what it is?

Adam: Strange you should ask me that this afternoon, I think that I was just about to ask myself the same question just as you walked in.

Gaynor: Fine, but can you answer it?

Adam: Well, it's obviously to do with concern for profits and its equally to do with concern for people and creating a climate where they can grow and develop.

Gaynor: That's rather vague.

Adam: Well, let me go on, sir. If it's to do with concern for profits then it is also to do with knowledge of modern management methods and techniques and how to use them. If it's to do with concern for people, then it's also to do with knowledge of human behaviour and its applications.

Gaynor: You're struggling, Adam, I remember we talked about the purpose of business[1] and it must lead on from there. We agreed that this was the satisfaction of the needs, wants and desires of those who control the business and generally, but not always, this involved a certain level of profitability. Now purpose must define or set the aims and objectives. Subsequently the policy indicates the means as to how to accomplish these. Policy acts then as the firm guide in all decision making at an operational level. Management, therefore, is the implementation of policy to achieve company aims and

[1] CS Chapter 12

objectives. Yes, I rather like that—I must remember to use it again.

Adam: I know you won't mind Mr. Gaynor, but I can't agree with you.

Gaynor: Go on then, I am not very busy at the moment.

Adam: I don't disagree with what you say, but really I am concerned with the assumptions which are being made. Indeed, the business purpose sets aims or objectives but this implies that the business purpose has been established, is commonly perceived and is accepted. You next assume that policy is rationally formulated and promulgated, that managers are aware of it, and take their decisions within its limitations.

Gaynor: Perhaps that describes the ideal situation, but I would still maintain that what I said—what was it—management is the implementation of policy to achieve company aims and objectives, is a good description.

Adam: May I ask what policy Mr. Hedges offended?

Gaynor: Ah well, now there are several. First it is unethical; second, if it became known it would damage our image and create havoc in staff relationships, and there are more besides.

Adam: But Mr. Hedges took a decision, presumably with a knowledge of the policies you mention, whose effects could militate against our aims and objectives as well as damage his career.

Gaynor: And a damn fool he was, too!

Adam: Were it a less serious affair, and something which was only a minor departure from Company policy, I can't help wondering how he or we would know that a departure had occurred. For example, if a manager gave 11% commission to travel agents during the winter to obtain some preference from them, would this be stopped if you became aware of it?

Gaynor: I hope that he would have discussed this with me first, but I can appreciate the point. After all we must be flexible enough to deal with special situations.

Adam: Doesn't this, then, highlight the problem of what we mean by policy? Earlier you said that policy acts as a firm guide, but payment of commission is pretty well fixed at 10% although you would be prepared to consider exceptions. I hope I am not splitting hairs if I suggest that our policy is to pay commissions, a procedure has been established which fixes this at 10%.

Gaynor: I think, in this case, you are tending to split hairs but I see what you are getting at; a confusion exists between policy and procedures. I must admit that I have confused these at times, yes I see the point—policy should act as a guide. But formulating policy in this way must make it so general that it cannot provide much of a guide, a paradox in fact. Another thought that occurs to me is that if the policy is to be an effective guide it should be written out and available for the manager to consult. I must say that this would be an unenviable task!

Adam: Reading text-books about management I have found the exhortation to have a written policy a common theme. I have never actually seen one so far for an hotel and one can appreciate why this is so. At the same time I would think it comparatively easy to spell out some policies; in the financial areas, for example, this would seem a fairly straightforward exercise.

Gaynor: Yes, and I think it could be done in the operating area too. I must admit, though, that I am not sure that I would like to have an exhaustive written policy document. I feel it would be a restriction on me.

Adam: I believe this is a fairly common feeling among senior executives; Glacier Metal Company introduced a written policy and their experience was that flexibility *increased* since when a change had to be made, everybody could be informed and a written amendment incorporated. This makes sense to me, but I have always had a sneaking feeling that they wrote a procedure manual rather than a policy handbook.

Gaynor: So you are back to your distinction between policy and procedures! Am I to take it, then, that you are advocating that we should try to produce a policy document for the Company?

Adam: No. sir, I may tend to overstate the case, but I would think that the existence of such a document represents a failure of management. At a unit level, and indeed at company level, it is essential to have *procedure* manuals since these provide a means of establishing and maintaining standards as well as a basis for training. I would also say that it is essential for a company to spend a lot of time clarifying its objectives and aims at the top level. The real problem is that many so-called policy documents are little more than a public relations handout. If a company is clear about what it wants to be, surely it should make every effort for everybody to understand and accept these aims and behave in a supportive way towards them.

Gaynor: I would have thought that having a written policy would help to do this, since people could see just what the aims are and act accordingly.

Adam: I am sure that this is partly true, but what I am trying to say is that if, starting at the top, members of an organization demonstrate by their behaviour what the policy is, this will be reflected downwards. If the senior executives behave as though they believed the customer was important, then other employees will adopt similar behaviour.

Gaynor: In other words, people will learn by example; I am rather intrigued that you should have such a charming old-fashioned idea!

Adam: By example, yes. But it is a little more than this. Put into the jargon, I would say that it is minimizing corporate discrepancy. That is, reducing the difference between what a company as a collection of people say, and what in fact they do.

Gaynor: Very well, I agree with what you say but I must say there are some grave dangers of misinterpretation. If the conclusion without the supporting argument is adopted it can become an excuse for avoiding the necessary analytical thinking at the top level. We seem to have strayed a long way from my attempt to define management; taking into account all you have said we still have a good description.

Adam: I agree, but the whole problem of vocabulary in management continues to be a stumbling block. I always remember a lecturer at college who said at his first lecture to us that he had to devise a vocabulary to talk to us which we would automatically adopt, but never to attempt to use it outside. Since there is no generally accepted or defined vocabulary he had to fashion his own to communicate with us. We all forgot, of course, and it took some time to stop using our private language when we went into industry.

Gaynor: You still forget sometimes!

Adam: Sorry! If we do understand that policy and company aims and objectives are in some way related to individual interpretation, depending on the perceptions of the people involved, then I think it is a good *de*scription. But shouldn't a definition of this sort be a *pre*scription? By saying what it is, it gives some indication of how to do it?

Gaynor: Description, prescription, you're chopping words again. I will accept, although I think you are trying to find a philosopher's stone if a definition can tell a manager how to do his job!

Adam: To come back to the definition, sir, suppose the policy is wrong or the aims and objectives are wrong. Is it true to say that an individual is managing if he keeps things going to achieve these and doesn't have the wit or the insight to besiege his superiors for a change of direction?

Gaynor: Ah! Now you are introducing value judgements about 'good' management and 'bad' management!

Adam: No Mr Gaynor. You will accuse me of sophistry again, but I would say that a person who is a manager is managing effectively. If he is ineffective, then he is not a manager.

Gaynor: Save me from quibblers! But do go on.

Adam: When I was in America I was given an assignment to collect together as many definitions of management as I could find. It really was a fascinating exercise but eventually I found myself in such a muddle that I could hardly think straight. The things that people have to say about this process, which hundreds of thousands of people go about for five days a week, year in and year out is amazing. The one that I remember, and considered the most banal of a very sad bunch, was 'Management is getting things done through people.'

Gaynor: Oh! I always considered that a truism.

Adam: Well, yes. But it doesn't advance our understanding. Bus conductors, waitresses and supervisors get things done through people—but they are not managers.

Gaynor: Very interesting; so you don't think supervisors are managers?

Adam: No. Managers are tacticians; that is they are the people who are once-removed from the actual operators who serve the food or make the beds. Managers are concerned with the deployment of resources. A manager *says* what has to be done, a supervisor frequently *shows* people what has to be done. The supervisor is a technician, the manager is a tactician. In this sense he is *always* 'getting things done through other people' and the other people are his supervisors.

Gaynor: Well then why does this 'getting things done through other people' grate on you so much?

Adam: Chiefly because of its lack of prescription. Would you say that a person is an effective manager who spends all his time with his supervisors, guiding, instructing, directing and giving decisions?

Gaynor: No, certainly not. I would expect him to set the guide lines—policy, if you like—and by his selection and development of the supervisors, reach a stage where they got on with the work and left him time to think.

Adam: Exactly. I think it has been sufficiently demonstrated from studies of managers' and supervisors' behaviour that these are very different roles. We must be careful, however, about actual titles that go with a job.

Gaynor: Yes indeed. It was always a source of amusement to me, when I had the title of General Manager, to sit next to people, with the same designation, at conferences who ran an hotel with twenty bedrooms. I would be the first to insist that we belonged to the same industry, but our needs and problems were vastly different! Do we have any common ground, I wonder? The other thing that concerns me is the entrepreneurial aspect. The owner of a twenty bedroom hotel is an entrepreneur, whereas Kimble at the Diana is a manager employed by the Company. Yet he is responsible for about twenty times the turnover of this entrepreneur!

Adam: I have often pondered about this. In many ways it is a very personal thing. Occasionally I meet people who ask me why I work for Gaynor Hotels when I could be my own boss running a small hotel in the Cotswolds and probably able to take each afternoon off for golf. But it really depends on what you mean by being one's own boss. I am sure there is great satisfaction in being personally involved with the customer in the small business, but the real boss is then the bank manager and there is a very real dependence on suppliers. I think that one can over-emphasize the differences between the entrepreneur and the manager. Probably the owner of a small hotel spends about five per cent of his time on entrepreneurial decisions and the rest of the time he is a manager. So Kimble and the proprietor have a 95% of common activity if they are running similar establishments.

Gaynor: I suppose I am the professional entrepreneur of this Company, but I have never been able to find any courses which deal with this topic! But we are still groping about. You have the advantage of your research on definitions of management, what are your conclusions? After all, people like me that just manage, what time do we have for all this introspection?

Adam: Now I am in difficulties! On the one hand I am asked to offer my conclusions against your experience, and on the other hand I am asked to sit in judgement on the multitude of writers on management!

Gaynor: I thought this is what you did anyway, but please! You know that I want to know about your ideas and that I shall use my experience to challenge you where I think you are wrong. I know that you will produce research findings, that I have never heard of, like rabbits from a hat. But I am still interested in your ideas.

Adam: Sorry, Mr. Gaynor, but I just realised the enormity of what you asked me to do. It is one thing to make comments about a definition that somebody proposes; it is quite another thing to be asked, from limited experience, to fly in the face of the savants!

Gaynor: I quite understand, but go ahead.

Adam: Well, the early writers about management became heavily involved in trying to define management but I think because they were engineers or technologists, they wanted it cut and dried. They saw the world in mechanical terms and placed all the emphasis on what should be done to create orderliness and an organization which works like a smoothly oiled machine.

Gaynor: Then the social scientists came along and started to demonstrate that most of the problems were centred round people who did not behave like machines. In fact they were unpredictable.

Adam: Yes, but I think that the success of techniques in advertising show that there are quite a lot of predictable elements in people's behaviour. But the effect of the behavioural scientists findings tended to tip the balance with a lot of managers from concern for production to concern for people. In fact I sometimes think this still persists today to a large extent; from the way some people talk, one would think that the Hawthorne experiments[1] were the only studies which have been conducted in this field.

Gaynor: You mean that a manager should be involved in maintaining a balance between his concern for people and for production?

Adam: Yes. This means that management is a process which involves achieving business goals while at the same time providing a means of satisfaction for the individual needs or goals of employees. Now I think that the real danger to maintaining this balance might be described as the return on invested time. A comparatively short time spent in replanning a layout of a kitchen, or the desirability of installing a room state indicator can quickly produce economies. We can see that more meals can be produced or customers allocated rooms speedily. But to increase people's effectiveness, requires a much greater investment in time to establish what goals they are seeking to achieve.

Gaynor: I think most managers would agree with you and that they appreciate the need for developing people, but there is always the pressure of other things to be done and the consequent shortage of time. And what about decision taking, I would think that this is a basic and fundamental part of managing?

Adam: The problem of time is something I would like to come back to. I must admit that I feel slightly nervous when decision taking is regarded as some prerogative of managers. After all, everybody is involved in taking decisions every day. A housewife faces a major problem in a supermarket when she has to decide between paying 28p for a family-sized pack of detergent or 32p for a special large size accompained by a free plastic flower!

Gaynor: I see what you mean, but surely we cannot divorce this business of making decisions from a process of management? I keep reading that use of computers is likely to remove a lot of decision taking from middle management in the future. But I don't think this will come for a long time and I certainly think that in running hotels there will continue to be a lot of decisions which would defy any computer. We will still need the reception manager who can fit an unexpected regular customer into the hotel which the computer says is full.

[1] see Brown, J A C *Social Psychology of Industry*, Penguin, 1954, Chapter 3, The work of Elton Mayo.

Adam: Yes indeed, we cannot ignore that decisions have to be taken in business organizations and it needs some careful thinking to distinguish between normal human decision taking and the special characteristics of those in business.

Gaynor: That should not be too difficult. I am sometimes very conscious of spending time collecting information in order to make a decision. In a similar way, you or the chief accountant sometimes spend time preparing briefs about the possible alternatives available and the likely results. A lot of this involves figures and projections and so on. With no disrespect to you, most of this could be done better on a computer, but I will still have to make the decision about which line to follow. I would also think that the unit managers will have to continue making similar decisions; perhaps these are less important in that a wrong one will be unlikely to damage the company, whereas mine might! In these decisions, at both levels, we have to use experience and our personal judgement.

Adam: If most of the operating decisions at unit level are to be made by computers in the future, the managers' role becomes one of a human relations mechanic.

Gaynor: I don't see it that way. I hope that they will use information from the computer in reaching operating decisions; I suppose I am agreeing with your balance between people and production. My concern, however, is that this is the only method I can see for developing executives. As you know, we are a fairly decentralised company and I want my managers to feel that they are more than what you call 'human relations mechanics.' This really goes back to what I was thinking earlier when I used the word 'policy'. One would like to feel, as a company, that decisions are made in accordance with the policy and this is the paradox you saw. I am reluctant to start writing everything down, but I do want decisions made which support what we are trying to be as a company. Perhaps it would be a better way of describing this to say that I would like to create an ethos or spirit that ensures this.

Adam: I would say that creating this environment or ethos is a very important part of the management process. It can probably be compared to the training we have as children; having confidence in social situations because we have a good idea of what is the 'right thing to do' like not putting our elbows on the table.

Gaynor: I thought only great-aunts worried about that nowadays! But I think you have something. Tell me, where does problem solving come into all this? I certainly seem to spend a significant part of my time dealing with problems and I am sure it is the same with all managers.

Adam: Just before you came in I was thinking about this; after a year I am still involved in solving problems and I find this rather disappointing.

Gaynor: This is what I mean. Surely you can't expect problems to stop requiring solving, I would think that this is almost the core of what management is about.

Adam: This makes me feel uncomfortable. Identifying problems and solving them certainly is a significant part of managing. But I can't help feeling that this is catching hold of the wrong end of the stick. Surely if we concentrated on identifying the *causes* of problems and removing those we could be much more effective?

Gaynor: I am not sure I understand you.

Adam: Perhaps I can illustrate it with the problem we had at the Apollo.[1] Rather, I should say, problems; no potential managers were being produced, there was a high labour turnover and so on. We could have attempted to solve these by introducing different methods of selection, higher pay and various other means. These might have had some effect but in the long run we hadn't identified and remedied the cause. That was Whitstone, whose autocratic behaviour as a manager was the cause of the problems.

Gaynor: Yes, I see what you mean. It is like worrying about the problem of high labour costs at Head Office when the cause is people wanting to have things in writing as a protection.

Adam: Exactly. But having said that, I am not sure just how this fits in with the management process. Undoubtedly managers are involved in solving problems and now it sounds as though I am saying they shouldn't be.

Gaynor: From what you say, and it is certainly a new slant for me, I would see this as part of the ethos. It involves analysing the cause of problems rather than saying 'we have a problem'. This reminds me of one of the British Institute of Management's luncheons when Peter Drucker spoke. It was very impressive to me when he said something like 'We are concerned with effective management rather than efficient management, because a manager can be very efficient at doing something that does not need to be done'. I remember that I was disturbed for several days afterwards!

Adam: This really typifies how one can see a whole new dimension to the task of managing by taking a step sideways and looking at the words we use. I sometimes think that words and cliches are like old slippers, they are comfortable until you notice the holes in them.

Gaynor: Comfortable, but not presentable! What about communication? I recall that we have said something about this before.[2] It must come in somewhere.

[1] CS Chapter 4
[2] CS Chapter 8

Adam: I think on that occasion you quoted Thoreau and said, 'How can I hear what you say, when what you are keeps drumming in my ears'.

Gaynor: Ah yes! A favourite quote of mine.

Adam: Well, the way I see it is that if your ethos exists, then communication will occur. Most people in talking about communication generally emphasize the skills of writing, speaking and reading. Sometimes they also include the skill of listening. These are, of course important, but I would think that the emotional and social context are important. Which is just what Thoreau was saying.

Gaynor: So you don't consider communication is a part of managing.

Adam: Oh, I think it is, but if we mix Drucker with Thoreau and add a dash of your observation on the ethos of the enterprise, we can see that communication is a function of the internal environment. If trust exists and people appreciate the objectives, then communication will occur. If not, then no communication.

Gaynor: In some ways I would describe it as 'good' and 'poor' communication, but I am a little worried that you might take me to task on these words! Look, I have a lunch appointment and must go in a few minutes. This has been a very interesting discussion, what shall I do, sum up what we have been saying or leave it to you to prepare a memo?

Adam: I would rather you summarized, Mr. Gaynor. After all, I don't want to land myself with solving a problem of overloaded Head Office typists!

Gaynor: Your motives are suspect, but let me see. The Management Process seems to be concerned with creating an environment in which a balance between concern for production and concern for people is maintained as well as providing a guide to decision taking. It is directed towards an analysis of the causes from which problems arise and seeks to provide for achievement of organizational objectives whilst satisfying individual needs. Is that adequate?

Adam: It really is a concise statement of what we have been talking about.

Gaynor: Does it satisfy your demands for prescription?

Adam: I think it does because it stresses the things that a manager must do. Creating the environment, for example. But I wonder how long this takes to achieve.

Gaynor: You have a chance to find out, Adam. Tell me about it when you come back from the Zephyr! Goodbye for now, and enjoy yourself.

2

A SPELL AT THE HELM

Suit the action to the word, the word to the action
SHAKESPEARE

Adam sat back in his chair on the first morning after returning to head office from the Zephyr. There was a note from Gaynor inviting Adam to his office later in the morning. Adam reflected that Gaynor would probably want to talk about his experience over the last six weeks of running the Zephyr.

He looked round his office with an affection which comes from familiarity and happy associations. Adam chuckled to himself in anticipating his meeting with Gaynor and opened the first page of the diary he had kept as a reminder of his adventure.

*

April 3rd. It's now four days since I have taken over and only seems like a matter of hours. The staff seem to have accepted me well, particularly the department heads. However, after my first speech to them when I arrived, have not really had the chance to talk to them individually. The hotel does not seem to have any real problems and we have been running at ninety per cent occupancy all week. Not bad. Must spend time talking to each of them—I want to do a thorough examination of the operation and develop a sound profit plan for the rest of the year. Want to talk to the department head about their own performance on the job and what they can expect from, and have to look forward to with, the company. I noticed that all the cups in the coffee shop are chipped—must check on it. Burns, our bank manager, rang and asked if I will talk at the Rotary lunch next Tuesday on 'The Romance of Hotelkeeping'. Said yes. Saw Maggie Smith, a cleaner. She was fired and wants her job back. She is pregnant. She says she was asked to take down all the pictures in the front lobby and wipe the frames. Says she asked for help and the housekeeper fired her. Will check with the housekeeper, whether alternative job offered.

Night auditor has not balanced for two nights; why is he allowed to go home without balancing? Must check on it. Must also check the worn carpet on the second staircase—it's threadbare and looks terrible. Dinner in the restaurant was excellent tonight. David Jones, our main meat supplier, joined me. Must tell the chef. Persuaded

Jones to improve on the ribs of beef we are getting—they have not been to specification lately. At least, so the chef tells me.

April 6th. Spent the morning with Mr and Mrs Fairweather. Their daughter is getting married in August and I booked the reception. Very good price agreed and am quite pleased with myself. Did not want to bother Gripple, my assistant manager, with it. Had asked him to review all of our marketing commitments and contracts for this coming summer and give me a report. Am quite pleased with Gripple, he is a competent young man and am sure we were right that he is not quite ready to be 'top dog'. Saw the housekeeper in the afternoon. She said that Maggie Smith, the ex-cleaner, was offered a job as ladies' powder room attendant and she refused. Must make sure this is documented. We had a long talk. She is a pleasant woman but completely obsessed with repairs and maintenance. Says that two thirds of the work orders are outstanding at this moment and have not been attended to. Am going to check some rooms with her in the next few days. The five people came in for an inspection and they seem satisfied. The night auditor finally balanced last night. Gripple said that he had had a quarrel with his girlfriend who doesn't like him working at night. Let's hope he's all right now. Colonel Smithey, who travels around selling gin, came in to make my acquaintance. He's been staying at the hotel for ten years now and was at school with Gaynor. Pleasant man. Bought him two or three drinks and joined him for dinner. Saw Grayson, the chief engineer, earlier. He controls the repairs and maintenance budget as well as the capital expenditure budget for all areas. Asked him about the carpet on the second staircase. He tells me that it's not in this year's budget.

April 10th. Have been working on revised profit projections. Have decided that I will do them first, then have each department head review them and comment. Better to do it this way than have the department heads too much involved at the start. They have never done profit projections before and wouldn't know where to begin. Had a department head meeting and told them what I was doing. Not much response. Lot of complaints, however, about all sorts of things: shortage of teaspoons, staff coming in late, food being left out in the kitchen, the delivery yard being filthy, two staff required on duty when they should have been playing for the football team, too many mistakes on the salary cheques, waiters using napkins as shoe cloths. I gave up taking notes. However Diana, Gripple's secretary, gets the minutes down very capably. She's also very cynical. Says the same things come up every meeting ever since she has worked at the Zephyr. Had a questionnaire from somebody carrying out a survey on hotels. That's the second one this week. Will have to put somebody on the staff specially if we are to participate in all these surveys! Kent, our chief accountant, is a strange man, he always seems to be avoiding me. Have not sat down and talked to him yet.

April 12th. Nearly the whole day spent on the case of June Wakes. She is one of our two bar waitresses in the Cowboy Bar. Very popular with guests—a blonde with lots of personality and a very good manner. The housekeeper saw her coming out of a bedroom with one of our regular travelling businessmen and came to see me about it. I talked to the girl. She didn't deny anything and just said that she had been friendly with the man for a long time. She said she was very sorry, that she had been off duty, that it wouldn't happen again. The real problem was that Gripple told me that the housekeeper had reported her two months ago for spending the night with the Star King, a singing celebrity. The Star King had been giving two performances in the town and had stayed at the hotel. Anyway Hedges, the former manager, had been so pleased with the public relations from the Star King's visit that he had just laughed the whole thing off. So if she hadn't been fired then why should she be fired now? Decided to call a fast department head meeting and put it them. They all voted to fire her except Carter, the chef. So I called her in later and told her she was fired. She cried bitterly and she really is sorry about it. She is separated from her husband, lives with her mother and has a two year old daughter. Also she has done a very good job for us in the past. Decided to re-install her. Called another fast department head meeting and told them of my decision. Didn't exactly say that they were bigoted but I certainly thought it.

April 15th. Maggie Smith, the pregnant ex-cleaner, came to see me again. Had I talked to the housekeeper—could she have her job back? I told her that she was fired and would stay fired. Something about her attitude that I just didn't like. I realise that with Hedges going, my stepping in, and another manager taking over soon, the department heads must be a bit uneasy. Decided to give a cocktail party for them next week. I want to involve Kent, the chief accountant, on these profit projections now that I have made a good start on them. Our lunch sales are down badly compared with last year. I'm sure it's the menu. Talked to the chef and asked him to come up with some new ideas. The hotel is still very busy, we have ninety three per cent occupancy for the month to date. That's well up on last year.

April 23rd. Checked ten bedrooms this morning. They all seem to have things wrong with them and I had the housekeeper waving work orders at me which go back three months or more. Must talk to Grayson, the chief engineer. Kent, the chief accountant, has had my profit projections for over a week now, must ask him what he is doing with them. Heard from Gaynor that the new manager is appointed—a woman, times are changing. She is coming on May 12th and I will leave on May 15th. Looked at Gripple's report on marketing commitments and contracts. Some strange contracts have been negotiated in this place and the room rates agreed are far too low. Sometimes I wonder if we need to have these low priced contracts with tour operators at all. Problem is that we don't have enough information to answer that. Missed out on dinner because Gripple took his mother out, together with the only key to the cellar. I had to take the hotel car and go and find him. What does one do when the bar runs out of vodka? Must talk to Gripple tomorrow about the requisitioning system.

April 26th. Spent the morning talking to Grayson. He is a man of about sixty who is basically a plumber. He does seem knowledgeable about most technical things but he has no system whatsoever in his department. 'I know everything that needs doing', he kept saying. 'I know, I get round to it as quick as I can'. 'She' (referring to the housekeeper), wants everything done at the blink of an eyelid. Well she can't have it can she?' It seems that we have the cheapest car parking in town, nobody has thought of reviewing our rates for years. Will ask Gripple to look into it. Cocktail party for the department heads in the evening. Seemed to go quite well. If anything the wives were more relaxed than the men. The housekeeper's husband, however, was a real live wire. He finished up playing the piano and played it very well indeed.

April 27th. In reflecting on our department heads' cocktail party last night, I am wondering whether we have the appropriate departmentalisation. With an assistant manager, chief accountant, head chef, restaurant manager and housekeeper, it seems about right. I don't really believe that a general manager should have more than five people reporting to him. Whether these are the right five or not is another matter. For example, we have no food and beverage manager, as such. We need to think more carefully about the whole subject of the organisation to do the job. Spent a couple of hours talking to Gripple about market information systems. He's quick on the uptake and completely followed the necessity of obtaining vital market information. He is going to go back on the reception records and analyse the business generated by travel agents last year. How many room nights (one occupied room for one night) and which agents gave us the most business. It's a start anyway. Got the profit projections back from Kent, the chief accountant. No comment made by him other than he agrees with them. I have now listed the specific costs on which I want him to comment and have sent them back to him. Had a long talk with Blakeney, restaurant manager,

who is also in charge of the coffee shop, bar and the Cowboy Bar.
He is very much an old timer but a good man. Am delighted to say
he gets on very well with the chef and they seem to work as a team. I
would like to see Blakeney become much more closely involved with
selling banquets. The general manager of the Zephyr has always
done this himself which is ridiculous. Or is it? I am not quite sure
who might best do it. The housekeeper came in to thank me for last
nights party and asked if I had done anything about Grayson, the
chief engineer. I am not quite sure what she expects me to do. Fire
him?

April 29th. Had a long talk with Kent. Asked him about the
planned profit projections. Also why he always seems so hesitant
and diffident. He finally seemed to relax and became quite expansive
in the end. He is very much a book-keeper. He balances and reports
figures but he doesn't have any inclincation to analyse them. He has
never been asked before to comment on the hotel's profitability and I
think I got him quite excited about it. I'm sure that he is capable of a
great deal more than has ever been asked of him. Had a letter from
the local technical college asking for a copy of the talk, I gave at the
Rotary lunch, on the romance of hotelkeeping. The month to date
figures are incredibly good. We should finish the month well up on
April of last year. All the costs are improved too, when looked at as
percentages of revenue. Gripple asked if there might be an opening
for him at head office. He says he doesn't want to stay on and work
for another general manager at the Zephyr. Persuaded him to stay
on, for the sake of continuity, for another six months. Then I may be
able to do something for him. First day for our new luncheon menu.
However, I forgot to do any local advertising and, of course, nobody
else thought of it!

May 2nd. Had the new carpet laid on the second staircase. It
looks very nice indeed. This hotel is certainly making enough money
to afford a few yards of new carpet. I don't know how it ever got left
out of the budget. Had a department heads meeting and
congratulated everybody on the April financial results. Not much
response except from the housekeeper who talked for ten minutes on
what a difference I had made to the hotel. She seems to believe that
sycophancy is part of surviving. Still perhaps it always worked for
her. She has been at the Zephyr now for about ten years. Am
shocked at the excessive use of the photocopying machine. Have had
a book started so that a note of everything copied has to be made
and signed by the person responsible. The steak I had for dinner last
night was terrible. Talked to the chef about it. It seems that the batch
of steaks in question should never have been accepted when
delivered. He had been at the dentist and the storeman had signed

for them. The chef had no other steaks in the kitchen so he was forced to serve them since the menu had already been printed. He was disappointed that I hadn't commented on the new luncheon menu. I thought that I had done. Not really sure what to do about Grayson, the chief engineer. He assured me that all repairs and maintenance work was up to date during the course of the department heads meeting this morning. However, I know that the situation is just as bad as it was before. Tom Minks, who has the jewellery shop in the High Street, was in the hotel. Told him that he should have a showcase in our front lobby and, to my surprise, he agreed. I did not, as yet, get down to negotiate a rental figure with him.

May 3rd. Not much unusual today. Got my profit projections back from Kent with a few useful comments.

May 8th. Uneventful day. Don't seem to be getting round to keeping up this diary. Somehow seem to be too busy on other things.

May 12th. Miss Shepherd, the new manager arrived. Seems a very talented person. Called a department heads meeting and introduced her. The men seem surprised that they now have a woman as a boss. I will spend tomorrow with her and then leave the day after. I can easily hand over in a day and there's always Gripple if I forget to tell her anything. The sooner I leave the sooner she can take control and assert herself as the manager. Must finish off the profit projections for her.

May 13th. Haven't done the profit projections. I think it's pointless for me to do them anyway, Miss Shepherd is going to be running the hotel so she agrees that she would rather produce her own projections since she will have to live by them.

*

Adam closed the diary and put it down. He chuckled to himself—it was horrifying. If anybody else read this diary would they really believe that he, Adam, knew anything about management? 'But after all', Adam thought, 'I got results'.

3

A NEW MANAGER

Man, unlike any other thing organic or inorganic in the universe, grows beyond his work, walks up the stairs to his concepts, emerges ahead of his accomplishments.

JOHN STEINBECK

Later in the morning, after returning from the Zephyr, Adam went to Gaynor's office.

Gaynor: Hello, Adam, glad to have you back at head office again!

Adam: Good morning, Mr. Gaynor. I was just reflecting on the pleasant parts of being back and of the things I shall miss.

Gaynor: And what will you miss most?

Adam: What you might call 'being at the sharp end'; the drama, actually having contact with the customer, sorting out the problems as they arise. Mostly, various things actually happening. Being at head office has many rewards in its own way, such as the overview of the company and contributing to its development, in however a small way.

Gaynor: I must say I agree; perhaps we become a little remote here at head office and sometimes I think how little different it might be if we were selling tyres or electric toasters. Still, tell me about your experiences at the Zephyr; not the detail at this stage, we can go into that later, just your major impressions from your spell at the helm!

Adam: It certainly was an interesting experience and a valuable reminder to me about realities of the operational level! I was very conscious that my stay was only temporary and tried to be circumspect about any changes. It also brought home to me some of the personal or individual aspects of management. As an operator, I held Hedges in high esteem, but several things at the beginning seemed to be ripe for improvement. But I later became very aware, as I tended to lose the impetuous of novelty, how a routine develops and things either get overlooked or deferred. Of course there was a case of conflict between department heads and one individual who only needed a little encouragement to suddenly start to develop, a latent potential. We were right about Gripple, too; he needs more experience although he is a bright enough young man. He seems to be turning his eyes on head office—maybe it is the office hours which attract him. Just before I left we wondered how long it would take to create a particular environment; all I can say now is that it must take longer than six weeks! But it seems to me that about this length of time seems to be related to establishing a routine.

Gaynor: Well now, tell me how you found Miss Shepherd. I am only sorry that it was not possible for me to introduce her myself, but I had to go abroad. I formed the impression that she would be quite capable of presenting herself.

Adam: Indeed yes, sir. She really seems a most competent person and seems to know almost as much about the company as I do; she must have absorbed your briefing well!

Gaynor: I will admit, that when she came to see me, at one stage I began to wonder just who was interviewing whom! She had armed herself with a list of questions about our whole operation, and attitudes, that I found it quite exhausting—very enjoyable though to meet somebody with such an alert mind.

Adam: I am curious to know how you managed to find her, I can recollect no advertisements for the post. In fact, I once wondered if I would ever be replaced!

Gaynor: Now Adam, you know that you are needed at head office; during your absence I have come to appreciate how much I rely on you. Actually, the day after you left for the Zephyr I had this application to be considered for a managerial appointment with a covering letter to say that Miss Shepherd was looking for a new and demanding post. I was immediately impressed by the curriculum vitae which she sent and arranged an interview straight away. The rest you know. Have a look at the outline of Miss Shepherd's career, and you will see what I mean.

*

CURRICULUM VITAE

Name	Barbara Vesey SHEPHERD (Miss)
Home address	Hillview, Martin's Road, Seaville, Devon
Present address	Inchcliffe Hotel, Barley Row, London W.2
Date of birth	11th June, 1947
Place of birth	Yaxley, Nr Eye, Suffolk
Nationality	British
Religion	Church of England—Anglican

EDUCATION	Schools:
1952–1958	Myford Preparation School, Yaxley, Suffolk
1958–1963	St. Margaret's School for Girls, Goudstone, Sussex terminating in General Certificate of Education

	College:
1963–1966	Hotel and Catering Department, Seaville Technical College, Devon Course followed: Three year course in hotel and catering management terminating in the award of National Diploma.

Awards:
1964
Technical

Gold medal for Culinary exhibit, Torquay International Gastronomic Festival. Passed City and Guilds 150 examinations: Theory and Practical Basic Cookery for Hotels

Managerial

1st prize in country-wide 'Plan a Kitchen' competition organized by the Gas Council. Received the Silver cup for academic attainment at the end of the 1963/64 academic year.

1965
Technical

Passed the Hotel and Catering Institute's Intermediate Practical and Theory Restaurant Waiting Examinations
Passed City and Guilds 151 examination: Theory and Practical Advanced Cookery for Hotels. Received the Marius Dutrey Trophy for gaining highest marks in the country for the 151 examination.

Managerial

3rd prize in an essay competition organised by the Hotel and Catering Institute.
Received 2 Silver cups for academic attainment at the end of 1964/65 academic year.

1966
Technical

Passed the Hotel and Catering Institutes Final Practical and Theory Restaurant Waiting Examinations
Bronze medal for culinary exhibit, Torquay International Gastronomic Festival

Managerial

Passed Diploma examinations with distinction. Passed examinations for and awarded Associate Membership of the Hotel and Catering Institute. 1st prize in an essay competition organized by the Central Electricity Generating Board Awarded travelling scholarship by the Hotel and Catering Institute and Seaville Hotel Association.

1968
Managerial

Elected Member of the Hotel and Catering Institute: MHCI

EMPLOYMENT

1963–1966·   Whilst attending College periods have been spent working in the following areas:
Restaurant, Cocktail Bar, Kitchen, Control Office, Accounting Office and Catering Office.
Royal Hotel, Seaville, Devon
Hotel Waldheim, Waldheim, Switzerland.

Post College

Summer 1966   *Receptionist/Cashier: Royal Hotel, Seaville, Devon*

Duties and responsibilities   All aspects connected with administration of the Rooms Department of a 100 bedroom hotel. This included the various facets of reservation, sales, public relations and accounting in some detail.

Value of experience gained to personal development

Technical skills   Exposure led to a reinforcement of technical knowledge gained at College and much greater confidence in dealing with practical situations.

Managerial skills   The consciousness of the need to work effectively as a member of a group. The realisation that many systems and procedures employed were not beyond being questioned and challenged.

Winter 1966/67   *Receptionist/Cashier: Maine Beach Club, Nassau, Bahamas*

Duties and responsibilities   The same broad areas were covered as at the Royal Hotel

Value of experience gained to personal development

Technical skills   Knowledge of different systems and approaches adopted.

Managerial skills   The opportunities providing a chance to think about an optimum way of organising this area of an hotel and to start to make some generalizations about it.

Summer 1967   *Assistant Housekeeper: Hotel Maurice, Locarno, Switzerland*

Duties and responsibilities   Involvement with all aspects of a Housekeeping Department. From administration and leadership of the work force, to the full range of personal services offered, to the routine and non-routine maintenance of facilities.

Value of experience gained to personal development.

Technical skills	A great deal learnt from the application of technical knowledge in the practical situation.
Managerial skills	A greatly increased confidence in dealing with staff and guests. With particular regard to staff a great deal was learned about how, and how not, to motivate staff to work effectively. This became particularly clear in view of the fact that I was working with staff of different nationalities speaking a number of different languages.

Winter 1967/68   *Assistant Housekeeper: Maine Beach Club, Nassau, Bahamas.*

Duties and responsibilities	The basic administration of the Housekeeping Department but also, as is always entailed, a close collaboration with other departments of the hotel.

Value of experience gained to personal development.

Technical skills	Development of more than a departmental view of an hotel. A realisation of the totality of the operation and the inter-dependence of the various departments.
Managerial skills	Much more understanding of the network of personal relationships which constitute an organisation.

Summer 1968   *Receptionist/Cashier: Manitoba Inn, Ontario, Canada.*

Duties and responsibilities	Mainly concerned again with the administration of the front office areas.

Value of experience gained to personal development.

Technical skills	Again exposure to different systems and approaches creating an opportunity to compare and test ideas previously formulated.
Managerial skills	Complete confidence in quickly establishing the sort of personal relationship needed to be able to contribute rapidly to the effective running of a department.

Winter 1968/9	*Executive Housekeeper: Maine Beach Club, Nassau, Bahamas.*

Duties and responsibilities — Concerned with the complete operation of the Housekeeping Department.

Value of experience gained to personal development.

Technical skills — A rapid development of skills which only comes from assuming full operational responsibility for a department.

Managerial skills — A consciousness of the very great but not insurmountable difficulty attached to winning the wholehearted support of all members of staff.

Summer 1969	*Extensive Tour—Bahamas, Bermuda, United States, Mexico, Canada, Africa, Holland.*

This was the most broadening experience of my life; a kaleidoscope of different places, people and situations developed enormously my insights both into myself and into the world at large.

Winter 1969/70	*Reservations Manager: Salt River Inn, Phoenix, Arizona, U.S.A.*

Duties and Responsibilities — The complete operation of the front office.

Value of experience gained to personal development.

Technical skills — Finally the opportunity to implement my own ideas. This proved to me that I was not only able to conceptualise but to actually initiate and implement my ideas successfully through other people.

Managerial skills — Above all, in relation to the above, that dynamic management must innovate.

Summer 1970	*Under Manager: Inchcliffe Hotel, London, England.*

Duties and responsibilities — Working within a fairly informal organisation structure, a variety of duties and responsibilities as delegated by the General Manager. These included deputising for him in his absence.

Value of experience gained to personal development.

Technical skills — An increase in confidence in the analysis and refinement of the operation of all departments of the hotel.

Managerial skills — The development and use of an approach towards the planning and formulation of the future of an hotel.

Summer 1971 — *Under Manager: Towner Hotel, Bradford, England.*

Duties and responsibilities — Of a similar nature to the Inchcliffe Hotel but with particular responsibility for the selling and execution of banquets and functions.

Value of experience gained to personal development.

Technical skills — A rounding off of technical skills resulting in a deeper awareness of the working of each department. In this respect too, a clearer insight into an hotel as a total system.

Managerial skills — Some small modification of my behaviour enabling me to be much more effective in the role of co-ordinator or catalyst. The experience of a number and range of different managerial styles had, at this stage, given me much to think about.

Spring 1973 — *Manager: Inchcliffe Hotel, London, England.*

Duties and responsibilities — Full responsibility for the Inchcliffe Hotel, answering to Diamond Hotels Central Office.

Value of experience gained to personal development.

Technical skills — To recognise quickly the approach to adopt and arrive at the correct technical solution to a technical problem.

Managerial skills — In a similar way, the increasing ability to recognise the inter-personal problems which lead to organisational disruption. Additionally, the ability to work upon these problems with the individual concerned and with the group as a whole. My aims are to achieve a commitment to a common goal, to develop and motivate each person to his fullest potential and to maintain the organisation climate to make this possible. Finally, I am satisfied that successful 'business' operation is in reconciling the needs of the market to be served with the return on investment to be achieved.

Adam: It certainly is an impressive record!

Gaynor: What I find most intriguing is the reflective analysis which she has made on each appointment. One gets a picture of her eagerly acquiring experience with a clear idea of constantly moving towards a goal of managing an hotel. I must admit that my own career was never so clear cut to me, although of course, it was inevitable that I would run the company. On the other hand, I felt a little nervous at the idea of such a dedicated lady and suspected that she may turn out to be a rather dominating character, aggressively steering her whole life to achieve a deep rooted ambition. But not a bit of it, as you know from meeting her, she is vivacious, charming and, above all, seems to have had a lot of fun working in these different places.

Adam: Miss Shepherd certainly picked up things quickly at the Zephyr and commented on several improvements she wanted to incorporate. In fact, we were so busy talking about these, and our general philosophy of hotel operation, that there was little time left for much more than cursory mention of our working careers. Now I can see how she was able to take over with such ease. If I was sly, Mr. Gaynor, I might ask you about the criteria you used for this selection!

Gaynor: You are sly, Adam, and you are provoking me; but it was not just the pretty face! To start with, I am not sure I have any established criteria for selecting managers. Of course, there are some fairly basic things such as appropriate level of knowledge and experience. After all, we do not appoint very many managers since they don't seem to leave us or are promoted from other positions in the company. I would look for some demonstrated competence as a manager and, by talking to them, try to estimate how they would fit in the company and share its philosophy. I recognise that some outside help by a specialist might be useful, but I am arrogant enough to say, at present, that I should be able to assess the suitability of a unit manager.

Adam: I can see your point and it seems valid where the level of a candidate's experience and competence are obvious. What I do wonder about, is the more marginal case; the person who seems to be just about competent, but arouses perhaps a little doubt in one's mind.

Gaynor: It would be unrealistic to say reject doubtful cases; after all, we have recruited people at various levels who seemed to be mediocre and have really blossomed.

Adam: And we have had a few who didn't!

Gaynor: True, but we seem to have been right more often than wrong—and that surely is a good test of both management and a selection system. In Miss Shepherd's case, my predictions are that she will do well, only time will demonstrate whether I am right or wrong, and I have told her that.

Adam: It must be hard for Barbara—Miss Shepherd—to know she is under the Gaynor microscope!

Gaynor: Hm, but then, every manager must accept as a way of life that if they are not under my microscope, they will be under somebody else's!

4

SYSTEMATIC ANALYSIS

The highest wisdom has but one science—the science of the whole.

TOLSTOY

It was one of those days when Adam was in his office bright and early, he sat at his desk, emptied his brief case, lit a cigarette and looked into space. He would have loved a cup of coffee but it would be two more hours before one would materialise. He picked up a sheet of paper which was half covered with his own handwriting. He had been reading Peter Drucker the night before and one paragraph had struck him so positively that he had copied it out. He read it through again.

A piecemeal approach will not suffice. To have a real understanding of the business, the executive must be able to see it in its entirety. He must be able to see its resources and efforts as a whole and to see their allocation to products and services, to markets, customers, and uses, to distributive channels. He must be able to see which efforts go onto problems and which onto opportunities. He must be able to weigh alternatives of direction and allocation. Partial analysis is likely to misinform and misdirect. Only the overall view of the entire business as an economic system can give real knowledge.[1]

This pointed to one of the most frequently made mistakes, thought Adam. That well worn cliché of not seeing the wood for the trees still summed it up very well. The mistake was to treat things in isolation and detached from the whole. It was rather like a doctor expecting to successfully correct a disability in somebody's arm, without taking into account the rest of the body or the whole person with which he was dealing. This is often the tendency in hotels, to look at an operation in terms of a collection of individual departments instead of looking at it as a whole. After all, an hotel reception, for example, is not a meaningful entity; it is no more autonomous than an arm without a body. One could not make any sense of the reception without relating it completely to the hotel of which it formed a part. The question is not 'what is the reception trying to accomplish', the

[1] Drucker, P., *Managing for Results*. Heinemann.

question is, 'what are the aims and objectives of the hotel and how does the reception contribute towards them?' Unless the total hotel is used as a frame of reference, then everything said or done about the reception would be meaningless. It is impossible to say whether the receptionist should wear black coat and striped trousers or when check-out time should be set, or even how many receptionists there should be, without relating all of these questions to the hotel as a whole. Adam knew that this approach is seldom adopted. Too often departments were autonomous without any overall hotel policy having been determined. Consequently a loose collection of departments prevailed, each determining their own aims and goals and all going in different directions. Every time a department was used as a starting point, this was being encouraged. The starting point had to be the whole hotel, only then could individual departments, as composite parts, be examined.

Of course it all came back to policy again. The policy needed to be determined for the hotel and then to be translated in terms of departmental policies with sets of supportive procedures. Adam laughed to himself, he remembered the number of times that he had asked a question about a procedure such as 'Why do you turn down the beds at night'. The reply to this was invariable, 'Because that's the way things are done in a first class hotel' or, 'Because that's the way we've always worked'. Nobody had ever said to him 'It's a procedure based on departmental policy which, in turn, has been developed from the overall policy of the hotel'.

It seemed common sense that all this was true but then he had never really crystallised his thinking about it before. He supposed that most people just had a feeling about the type of hotel in which they were working. The problem was that each department head probably had a different feeling. It seems to come back to the same thing, everything determined in a detached and unrelated way, with no proper framework to evaluate the operation in an objective manner.

The evaluation of whether things were done properly, or otherwise, is decided in a subjective way based on personal preference and feelings. Adam chuckled again, even Gaynor did this, he recalled that he had often said to him 'I hate to see women behind the reception'. There was absolutely no basis for making such a statement. However, he could have said 'The indications are, in this particular hotel with the type of market which it is serving, that it would be contrary to the customers expectations to find the reception staffed with women'.

The other thing that encouraged a narrow and departmentalised approach to an hotel was the specialist himself. It was difficult to get the head housekeeper and catering manager to see the whole hotel as the only meaningful entity, when they were spending their lives within their own departmental boundaries. This was all the more reason to try to break down the boundaries and involve these people in discussions on the hotel as a whole, bringing them back constantly to the overall frame of reference. One had to try and compensate all the time for their tendency to be blinkered and over specialised in their approach. For example, for a simple thing like a new wash hand basin in the kitchen; to the accountant it might mean an item of capital expenditure; to the engineer a plumbing problem; to the sales manager an opportunity to talk of the most hygienic kitchen in town. To the company secretary it might mean conforming with legislation about food handlers; to the personnel manager it might mean an improvement in working conditions. In fact, however, it would mean all of these things. As Drucker said, the problem was to see the big picture, to look at that wash basin as part of a total system. A system with each part interlocked and making sense, one with the other. With this sort of approach a lot of the disharmony and incongruity which exists in many hotels could be eliminated. Discord can be created by such things as a beautifully dressed immaculate receptionist escorting a customer to a room which has a threadbare carpet; or a sumptuous Florida cocktail served in a cracked plastic dish; or bed linen changed every day with sheets that have enormous darns in them. All of these things need to be resolved. In the latter case, for example, according to the type of hotel and the market served, it might be quite acceptable to use darned sheets. But, in such an hotel, it would be unlikely that a daily change of linen would be necessary or expected.

What was needed was an approach to the analysis of the operation of a department which would enable a thoroughly objective and rational evaluation to be made. The policy of the hotel could be taken and translated into a departmental policy which could then be examined systematically by every facet of its operation. Above all, one would try to satisy the inter-relatedness which existed so that everything within the department was in harmony. Taking this further would ensure that the whole department was in harmony with the aims and objectives of the whole hotel.

With this in mind Adam took the housekeeping department as an example, and prepared the following:

CHECKLIST FOR THE SYSTEMATIC ANALYSIS OF THE HOUSEKEEPING DEPARTMENT

THE HOTEL

State the policy of the hotel specifying particularly the aims and objectives in terms of the market to be served and profit to be achieved

What is the segment of the market served?
Who uses the hotel?
What types of customers do they represent:
　　transient tourists
　　terminal tourists
　　permanent residents
　　family visitors
　　institution and special events visitors
　　travelling businessmen
　　organised tours
　　conventions
　　weekend escapists
What was the room occupancy over the last twelve months; express by month and by day of the week?
What was the average length of stay?
What was the average room rate?
What was the percentage of double occupancy?
Who does not apear to use the hotel?

FACILITIES

How many rooms are there?
How many with and without bathrooms?
How many double bedded, twins and singles?
Describe the bedroom decor, furniture and fittings
What state of repair are these in?
What, if anything, should be done to the rooms to better satisfy the market?
Would this enable any raising of the room rates?
Would it also enable the hotel to attract potential customers at present not using the hotel? If so, when and by how much would the occupancy be raised?

SERVICE

What personal services are provided:
personal laundry
valet: shoe cleaning
   pressing
   cleaning
turning down
early morning tea
baby-sitting
florist
secretarial
other
What are the overall arrangements for room service?
Are they separate from housekeeping?

CLEANING

Describe the daily cleaning of the rooms from the job procedure. This must include how often the linen is changed
What is the total estimated time for cleaning a room?
Describe the daily cleaning of the public areas from the job procedures
Describe the system and procedures for all cleaning other than daily

WORK FORCE

List the present staffing of the department by categories, numbers and basic wage
What is the basic working week?
How are staff scheduled? Give example schedule
How much, how often and by whom is overtime worked?
What were the total wages for the department over the last twelve months?
Show monthly totals
State monthly total wages as a percentage of room sales

LINEN

Describe the arrangements which exist for the laundering of linen
List the present circulating stock of linen by item and estimate its total value

List the reserve stock of linen by item and express its value, for the end of last month and for the beginning of the last twelve months

How often are inventories taken?

Itemize linen discarded as worn out over the last twelve months

Itemize linen losses over the last twelve months

Itemize linen purchases over the last twelve months

What was the cost of laundry over the last twelve months? Analyse by months

CLEANING SUPPLIES

Is there a standard for the consumption of cleaning supplies for each room occupied? If so, what is it?

Itemize the quantity and value of cleaning supplies issued over the last twelve months. Analyse by month

How often are purchases made?

How often are issues made?

Itemize amount and value of stock held by:
    chambermaids
    main store

CONTRACT MAINTENANCE

Is any contract maintenance for repairs or cleaning carried out:
    window cleaning
    carpets
    upholstery
    curtains
    bed covers

How is the work scheduled?

Itemize cost of the last twelve months

CLEANING EQUIPMENT

Itemize all heavy cleaning equipment held

Describe how it is maintained

List cost of repairs and replacements over the last twelve months

KEYS

Describe the system of pass keys which exists

What are the arrangements for their issue and control?

LOST PROPERTY

Describe the arrangements for the handling of guest's lost property

PURCHASING

Who is responsible for purchasing:
linen
cleaning supplies
furniture and fittings and
other major items of replacement or
capital expenditure
Describe how purchasing decisions are reached

COMMUNICATIONS

Describe the system of communications between housekeeping personnal and
Engineering
Reception
Hall Porter
Room Service
List all forms or reports, and attach examples, that pass between housekeeping and these departments

PRACTICE OR PROCEDURE MANUAL

Does a manual of practices or procedures for the housekeeping department exist? If so, attach one copy. If not, how are procedures communicated to the staff?

PERSONNEL

List job specifications, if such exist, for each category of staff
Describe arrangements for the selection of staff
Describe arrangements for the induction and initial training of staff
Describe if, when and how meetings are conducted with staff
Attach an organisation chart for the department, should one exist

PLANNED PROFIT

Attach the planned profit for the rooms department for the last twelve months

Attach actual profit performance and show variances

State how planned profit figures are determined and explain any variances

List items of replacement and capital expenditure for rooms and housekeeping for the last twelve months

Show the cost of repairs and maintenance for the last twelve months

*

Adam read through the checklist and placed it aside for typing. Although it had been prepared quickly, it would be adequate for the moment and could later be improved. He reflected that a completed checklist would reveal a great deal about any housekeeping department and the answers would probably provide a comprehensive picture of the operation. Adam pondered on the extent to which an accurately completed checklist could be used to evaluate a department by somebody who had not actually visited it; but use in this way would, quite justifiably, evoke an unhappy reaction from the department head involved. However, properly developed and tested, the checklist could be used to help a department head to systematically evaluate their own departments. Possibly this could be done jointly with the General Manager.

As Adam continued to think about his attempt at a systematic analysis, his initial satisfaction diminished. All it seemed to do, in fact, was collect information about various aspects of the operation of the department. Although this had some uses, it failed to show where any interrelatedness existed. There was no indication of the way in which all the information fitted together to provide a basis for action. Just how modifications or changes to facilities, service or processes could be undertaken to better achieve the aims and objectives *of the hotel* did not emerge.

In the case of shoe cleaning, no indication was given of whether this *should* continue where provided; nor was any indication given from the information of how many rooms a chambermaid *could* clean. However, Adam supposed, that in asking the questions at least a start would be made to finding an answer. Was it, he mused, the same starting point which had been triggered off when he had reread the paragraph from Drucker? It had stated that partial analysis could misinform and misdirect, that an overall view of the entire business was needed. In that case, would it be misleading to attempt a departmental analysis? Perhaps a similar analysis should be conducted from the whole hotel at the same time?

Adam whistled under his breath, he concluded that he would have to think about this much further.

5

LET'S TALK ABOUT BANQUETING

... the great question is, not whether you should resist change, which is inevitable, but whether that change should be carried out in deference to the manners, the customs, the laws, the traditions of the people or in deference to abstract principles and arbitrary and general doctrines.

DISRAELI

Gaynor went over to the sideboard in his office, took out a bottle of sherry with two glasses and turned to Adam:

Gaynor: Come on, its five thirty, the main business of the day is done. I think we can treat ourselves to a drink. It's an Amontillado, that's all right for you Adam isn't it?

Adam: Yes indeed, Mr. Gaynor.

Gaynor: Here you are, cheers! Now let's take a few minutes, while we drink our sherry, to talk about banqueting. You know, we become very involved and professional in dealing with reception, bedrooms, restaurants, and so on but we seldom think seriously about banqueting. It's about time we did. It's a department which always seems to escape close examination and I don't really know why this is so. I think it's probably because we view it as being peripheral to our main type of business. We seem to regard it as being an optional extra which is tacked on and we are grateful for any bit of money that is contributed to total sales. Consequently I feel that it tends to run in a very unplanned and haphazard manner even though we have a banqueting department in practically all of our hotels.

Adam: Well I am not sure if that is quite fair. I think that some of the banqueting we have is first class and has earned itself a very fine reputation. Of course this does depend on the calibre of the particular banqueting manager as well as the extent of the facilities. Where there is a lot of banqueting we tend to have a very competent man. Where it is a small department, then the general manager may be in direct control and then it may well get pushed a little to one side. I agree with you, however, that we have never really formalised our thinking on banqueting. We have no real policy or procedures so I agree that, as a company, we certainly leave a lot to be desired.

Gaynor: Yes of course. I don't even know why we call it

banqueting. As far as I am aware a banquet is feast or a formal dinner with speeches. A great many of the functions which we cater for certainly wouldn't qualify under that definition.

Adam: That is certainly true; meetings, fashion shows, conferences, exhibitions, dinner dances—there is a wide range in the types of function. However, I don't know that I object to 'banqueting'; it is a generic term which has grown to include all of these types. I certainly wouldn't like to see our 'Banqueting Departments' suddenly re-named 'Functions Departments'.

Gaynor: Perhaps not, but for a start I would like to see this classification of types of function, which you just started, carried further. We should know more accurately what these various types of function are which we provide. In various locations we ought to know how the demand varies between types of function. If we don't do this then I am unable to see how we have anything like the proper basis for planning our physical facilities for banqueting. For example, I don't believe we would need the same facilities if we were mostly catering for dinners as opposed to conferences. At the same time, I don't believe that we should divorce any consideration of the market for functions from the market for the total hotel. You once made a number of points about this.[1]

Adam: Yes, I also think it is very appropriate that we should be talking about banqueting now. It is evident that general social and economic trends point to an increase in the total demand for functions of all kinds. More recreational activity will mean more societies and organisations and this should be reflected in a demand for annual dinners, meetings and so on. More business activity should produce more sales meetings, seminars, conferences and so on. I think that one must say that indications are, on a long term basis, that banqueting represents a very exciting growth potential. What do you think?

Gaynor: I agree, what you have said is quite clear. In fact, this played a large part in drawing my attention to banqueting. I really want to have a good look at it. Why don't you do me one of your summaries of the main consideration? You know, sketch out a framework from which we can develop our thinking and decide on some action.

Adam: Fine, I'll work something up and let you have it.

Gaynor: As soon as possible please, Adam. I don't want it to stick at the talking stage. My secretary might start to think that we just sit in this office talking our lives away. Another glass of sherry before you go?

[1] CS Chapter 9

Adam: No thank you. I think I ought to go, I have one or two things to tidy up before I leave.

*

Adam prepared the following summary within the next two days.

BANQUETING—MAIN CONSIDERATIONS

THE MARKET

In each location we should assess the potential demand for functions according to the various segments of the market
We should analyse the banqueting business which has been obtained in the past and relate it to the total potential demand. We can assess, therefore, the extent to which we are successful in exploiting present market opportunities.
The next step should obviously be to determine what should be done to our facilities, food, service, etc., to better exploit the marketing opportunities which exist.

At this point, it should be re-stated that an hotel cannot be all things to all people. If it attempts to satisfy widely different markets and develops a number of different markets and with a number of different images, then the total hotel will eventually assume the lowest of these images. Thus a lower segment of the market can only be catered for if banqueting facilities are well segregated from the rest of the hotel. This would mean separate entrances, cloakrooms, foyers, toilets etc.

TYPES OF FUNCTION

These are basically ten in number

- [ ] dinners
- [ ] luncheons
- [ ] dinner dances (balls and buffets included)
- [ ] cocktail parties
- [ ] press receptions
- [ ] wedding receptions
- [ ] fashion shows
- [ ] exhibitions
- [ ] meetings and conferences
- [ ] conventions

Note: Convention has been differentiated from meetings and

conferences since the majority of delegates would be residential in the hotel. The term meeting or conference would be used when only a few, of those attending, would wish to stay in the hotel. This is an artificial distinction made for our purposes only; the terms convention and conference are virtually synonymous, 'convention' being normally confined to meetings of ecclesiatical or political bodies.

PHYSICAL FACILITIES

In the planning of new facilities or in assessing the adequacy of existing ones, it must be borne in mind that it is difficult to produce facilities which are equally capable of fully satisfying the needs arising from all of the above types of function.

As far as possible, however, flexibility should be provided so that facilities can be altered or modified to cater for all the types and sizes of function for which a demand is anticipated. In this sense banqueting facilities might best be compared to a theatre stage which is a skeletal basis enabling the creation of different scenes, settings and atmospheres according to the particular piece or play. As two plays might be vastly different in their requirements, so also would be an exhibition of industrial products as opposed to a gala ball. Where it is not feasible, or prohibitive by capital costs, to provide such flexibility one should concentrate on the type of function to which the physical facilities would best lend themselves. Whatever the case, however, the decision must be made in the light of the potential demand for the types of function represented by that segment of market under consideration. It would be pointless to say, 'we have a beautiful ballroom, therefore we will concentrate on dinner dances', if there were no demand in that location for dinner dances or, at best, only a seasonal demand.

In planning facilities for conventions it is clearly important that the capacity of the hotel in terms of the number of bedrooms matches that of other facilities. Establishing convention facilities for 600 people with 100 hotel bedrooms would be a case in point, unless collaboration was envisaged with neighbouring hotels. In the same case the provision of breakfast for 600 with a meeting for the same number immediately following would also require careful thought at the planning stage.

The following twenty aspects of physical facilities for banqueting should be given careful consideration in accordnace with the identified market:

  ☐ provision of flexibility by partitioning in order to be able to

- [ ] cater for a variety of different size groups. The most desirable permutation to be achieved should be revealed by an assessment of demand
- [ ] sufficient sound insulation to prevent any nuisance arising from noise
- [ ] provision of a reception area large enough to accommodate the maximum number attending a dinner
- [ ] provision of sufficient cloakroom and toilet facilities for the maximum number to be catered for at one time
- [ ] use of chairs that, apart from fulfilling other criteria, are stackable and easily moved
- [ ] use of a table system that is flexible, easily assembled, dismantled and moved
- [ ] provision of adequate storage space for partitions, tables, chairs and operating equipment such as china, glass, silver and linen, when they are not in use
- [ ] reconciliation of floor covering needs and the periodic provision of a dance floor. For example, if carpet is used, incorporating a removable panel with a dance floor beneath
- [ ] planning of a flexible lighting system with consideration given to spotlights, dimming, changes in light fittings etc. It should allow for the satisfaction of a variety of needs and changes in atmosphere
- [ ] consideration of the overall decor. Exploration of the possibilities attached to a basic neutrality with flexibility for the rapid creation of theme effects for various types of function. This might be achievable by the use of movable mirrors, pictures, screens, curtaining, motifs, chandeliers, statues, fountains etc.
- [ ] provision of adjuncts such as bars, band stand, dais, fashion show catwalk, press box etc. Consideration should be given as to whether these should be permanent fixtures or temporary, removable and capable of installation only as required
- [ ] consideration of needs regarding acoustics, telephone points, microphones, closed circuit television, projectors, instant translation facilities, tape recorders, epidiascopes, screens and record players
- [ ] consideration of air conditioning and ventilation requirements as well as provision of water, gas, electricity, etc. for exhibition stands
- [ ] provision of access for heavy exhibits for trade or industrial exhibitions
- [ ] provision of sufficient and appropriate changing rooms for extra staff, entertainers, toast masters etc.

☐ consideration of precautions against fire such as inflammable materials, exits, sprinkler systems, statutory requirements etc.

☐ planning of food and drink preparation and service areas; types of menu and food and drink requirements, quantities, routes to and from service points, equipment and layout to maximise product quality e.g. hot food, and labour productivity e.g. the number of covers per waiter

☐ consideration of needs for all small equipment. For example ashtrays (whether portable and standing and/or fixed to the wall and chairs), blackboards and easels, gavels, lectern, signposts, typewriters

☐ consideration of the needs for car parking. There should be sufficient capacity for the maximum number anticipated at one time, if not in the hotel garage then within easy access of the hotel.

☐ consideration of providing the equipment and flexibility for the possible alternate use of facilities for other than functions, e.g. concerts, boxing and wrestling matches, other indoor sports contests or competitions.

CO-ORDINATION AND CONTROL

The instruction sheet

An instruction sheet should be raised for each function and should include the following information as appropriate:

General

Date and name of the function
Type of function
Name of client, telephone number and address
Times
Numbers
Ladies present or not
Bankers or credit reference
Price per head and what it includes

Menu

Details of the menu with all special instructions clearly stated. Ideally each menu item should be cross referenced to the chef's file of standard recipes and/or portion sizes.

Standard recipes and portion sizes for all banquet menus and food items should be pre-determined by consultation between the banqueting manager, the chef, any catering manager and even perhaps the general manager.

Any special modification of the standard recipes and portion sizes can be specified in the instruction sheet. Their existence would clearly simplify communication between the banqueting manager and the chef and enable the former to know exactly the product which he is selling. They will also help to prevent the situation arising when both the banqueting manager and client are surprised by the food which actually appears at the table

Drinks

Details of all drinks and beverages required during the course of the function: sherry, cocktails, beers, table wines, liqueurs and brandy.

Clear instructions should be listed as to how consumption is to be charged; estimated quantities of specified items which are included in the price; what is to be paid for on 'as consumed' basis; cash sales.

Rooms

Details of the rooms to be used. Whether their use is inclusive in the overall price or whether a room hire charge is to be made.

There should be a cross reference to the planned layout of the room.
Details of standard layouts, or the layout specifically planned for this function, should be held at this time in the banqueting office.
Details of any measures to be taken to create a particular type of atmosphere. Whether any action is required during the course of the function to change or modify the atmosphere further; e.g. the introduction of props or the dimming of lights etc. Details as to minor rooms should also be included.

Arrangements for cloakrooms, special arrangements of changing rooms and whether for staff, entertainers or a bride and groom.

Speeches, entertainment

Details and times of speeches and events during the course of the function, toastmaster, orchestra, cabaret, etc.
Provision of food and drink for these persons; where and when to be served and how charged.

Other services

Details of flowers, novelties, menus, wedding cake, photographer, cigars, cigarettes, etc.

Special equipment

Details of special equipment which may be required, e.g. telephones, closed circuit television, projectors, record player, tape recorder, etc.

Staffing

Details as to the staffing required for each service point; cloakrooms, bars, waiters at reception, waiters for the meal, etc. A breakdown between permanent staff and casual staff required should be included.

CO-ORDINATION

The instruction sheet will provide the main tool for co-ordinating a function by following the sequence:

Banquet sold and all details transferred to an instruction sheet
Instruction sheet to department heads for either action or information

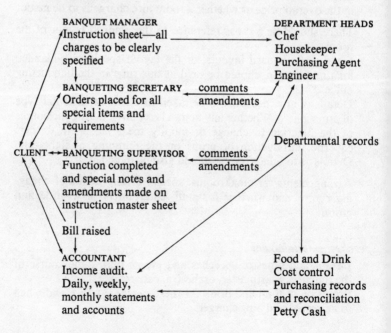

Banquet takes place according to instructions
Instruction sheet forms basis of the final bill to the client
Reconciliation of costs with revenue and planned performance against actual performance.

CONTROL

Control will relate to the particular system in use. In principle, the control procedure which should take place can be represented in the accompanying diagram.

Adam was soon in the position of having his efforts discussed by Gaynor.

Gaynor: Thank you for your summary, Adam, it has some good points. Incidentally, there is something I have been meaning to ask you for some time: when you tabulate things in your memos and reports, sometimes they are numbered and sometimes they have a symbol at the beginning. I have tried to identify a pattern in this because, knowing you, there must be some subtle reason.

Adam: Sorry, Mr Gaynor, I should have explained; when tabulated items are numbered it indicates that they have some sequential or ranking relationship. Often, however, tabulated items are simply points or factors to be considered which have no such relationship, then they are prefaced by a symbol.

Gaynor: Now I see! So here in your report you are saying that the twenty aspects of physical facilities for banqueting each need to be examined, but not necessarily in this sequence?

Adam: Yes, that's right.

Gaynor: I must say that I have never come across this before and I have read quite a lot about report writing.

Adam: My very own idea, Mr Gaynor!

Gaynor: Very well, that is sorted out. Now I would like to talk about what you have left out rather than what you included! Pricing, for example, is a vital consideration and I was surprised that you made no mention of it. The selling of banqueting is something else which you haven't included; selling a banquet isn't like selling a bedroom you know.

Adam: Well, I did think about both of these things and only decided to leave them out for the moment. I do agree that they are both very important. Pricing must be designed to take advantage of any market opportunity which exists. A long ignored pricing problem is often at the heart of the question of increasing sales.

Gaynor: I would have thought that the main point here is that pricing has got to be in harmony with the total package being offered. What I mean is, that it must not conflict with the image. You cannot have an exclusive image at knockdown prices. The overall objective of pricing, however, is to maximize an hotel's share of the market on a continuous basis while maximizing its return on investment. This means that pricing has to meet all competition. At the same time it must adequately cover the costs of production.

Adam: The usual practice is to start with the costs, I mean the costs of production, then work up to arrive at a profitable price level, regardless of market conditions and the likely volume of sales.

Gaynor: That's hardly credible, Adam. None of our hotels know exactly what the costs of production are in banqueting. They know roughly what the cost of food and beverage is but we have nobody who accurately allocates all the labour costs and other operating expenses. These tend to be absorbed by the main hotel operation. Anyway, this is someting which I will come back to later. Now what worries me most about pricing is that there seems to be little in the way of a systematic approach to its determination. Pricing is too often on the same basis as an Arab street market. In other words you get what you can after summing up the prospect. You sit with the client and bargain, add a bit on here, take a bit off there and determine a price which he, as an individual, is prepared to pay. The amount of suspicion, resentment and general ill will that this is likely to engender goes without saying. After all you wouldn't go and buy a wrist watch this way, you would expect the price to be clearly indicated.

Adam: Oh yes, I believe that one should have a properly priced tariff to submit to prospective customers. On the other hand if the wrist watch which you wanted had to be made to your specifications then the shop would not be able to price it until they had submitted these specifications to the manufacturer. They would give you an approximate estimate subject to confirmation. I think that this must clearly be the same case with a lot of banqueting. However, there is no reason why one shouldn't have a selection of standard menus properly priced and appropriately presented. Menu items could even be priced individually so as to allow the client to put his own menu together and know in advance what it would cost. If he does have special requirements, then it will still take a little time to quote a price to him. Alternatively, a selection of main courses can be priced to include a first course and dessert. A selection of first courses and desserts could be provided to choose from; there are various ways in which it could be done. I don't see any difficulty in this.

Gaynor: Very good, but I would go further than this; it is not only the price of the menu which causes confusion, it is all the extras which have to be added on: printing menus, flowers, service charges, the toastmaster and so on. Then, worst of all, there is the room hire charges. What the client wants to know is what the whole thing is going to cost. Why not give him an all inclusive price? There is no reason why it can't be done.

Adam: Agreed, even drink consumption could easily be built into a package price. We know roughly how much various types of people drink in a given length of time before dinner; whether it averages one, two or three drinks per person, whether they drink a third or half a bottle of wine with dinner. It should be no problem to cost this out and build it into the price.

Gaynor: You mean to do this with drinks rather than the guest paying for what is consumed and then watching him have a heart attack everytime somebody asks for a refill? Well, I certainly agree that there is a need for inclusive prices like this, especially with something like wedding receptions, but there could be drawbacks. Still one can always deal with the exception; our aim must be to make clear to the guest, as quickly and impressively as possible, what the overall cost of the function is going to be. To return to room hire charges, I would only like to see them used when there is no catering attached to the function. It would be appropriate if only coffee or tea or a few drinks were involved, otherwise it should be built into the price. For heavens sake, when I eat in a restaurant I don't expect a rental charge for the chair to appear on the bill!

Adam: Yes and I also think that with a proper tariff we could guarantee stable prices over a given period instead of having sudden fluctuations as costs either rise or fall. In any case we shouldn't just be forecasting our sales, we should also be forecasting our costs by intelligent assessments of the markets in which we buy and the general economic trends.

Gaynor: Quite: another thing is that we should be wary of pricing too closely to our competition. We should assess very carefully what we are offering as compared to our apparent competition. It may be that we have a unique product, that one or more aspects of our package—either the food, the service, the facilities or the image—are incomparably more desirable to the particular customers we are trying to reach. In such a case it might prove very much more in keeping to make our price considerably higher than those of other establishments in the area. The worst game of all is to play follow the leaders, to pick two or three other establishments and set prices according to theirs. We must price in accordance with all the conditions and trends which affect our particular product and our particular market.

Adam: The same goes for 'loss leaders' or promotional pricing, which prices below cost on the assumption that vast increases in sales will result. The theory is that cost will then decrease proportionately and profits will result. This isn't likely to work in a banqueting department although it could be used as a minor tactic.

Gaynor: Such as, at a period of the day when there is always spare capacity in the banqueting facilities and when low prices could also mean excellent public relations.

Adam: Yes that could be one situation. A reduction in prices below those of the competition can mean either of two things: taking business from competitors, in which case they will reduce their prices too, or increasing the total market which means more people will start holding functions. If the latter is unlikely then the eventual outcome is that the total market has remained the same size whilst their needs have been catered for at considerably reduced prices. All that has been done is reduced profitability of all the hotels. Yes, this is very interesting.

Gaynor: Of course it is Adam. Now you see why I wanted you to consider pricing. Well what about selling?

Adam: What do you mean, actual selling techniques?

Gaynor: No, I would rather say the organisation and strategy for selling. You know the main problem here is that we have a banqueting manager who is expected to perform two distinct and separate functions: sales *and* production. He both sells the banquet and organises and supervises its production. Now quite apart from each of these areas being quite specialised and having different requirements from the point of view of skills and knowledge there is also the question of time, how can he be in two places at once? While he is supervising one function he may have prospective customers waiting around to see him. While he is interviewing a prospective buyer, the client at a banquet in progress is clamouring for his presence in order to take care of some query or other. No, I am increasingly convinced that we should separate the two functions. Perhaps there should be staff to concentrate on sales and staff to concentrate on production. Obviously it will depend on the size of the hotel in question but, wherever possible, we should try and organise the department along these lines. The trouble is that because tariffs are not formalised and because the banqueting manager carries most things in his head, he is the only person who can possibly do the selling. As I have already said, this is ridiculous. We have to formulate clearly the types of function which we are able to offer, what can be included in the way of food, service and so on, and what prices we will charge. We then have to train people, as well as the banqueting manager, to be competent at selling.

Adam: I see, there is also a lot of room for improvement in merchandising or presentation; in really impressing the client at the point of sale when the sales interview is taking place. So many times these interviews are conducted in a very unsatisfactory manner. In a crowded office with a typist banging away on her machine, with people interrupting and the telephone ringing and so on. Sometimes clients are even interviewed in the middle of the hotel lobby. This isn't the right way to go about selling. In conditions like these it doesn't matter how clever you are with your sales pitch you are not going to be successful.

Gaynor: Just so, a prospective client should be interviewed in a very smart and elegant office which should reflect the whole image of the hotel. There should be no secretary present unless she is there to take notes on the particular banquet being discussed. The client should be offered cigarettes, a drink or tea or coffee as appropriate. There should be illustrations or photographs of how the particular room looks when laid up ready for service. Photographs of floral displays, centre pieces, ice carvings, wedding cakes and so on. Every device must be used to try and *show* the client what he can actually expect to get. Why not have a display cabinet with examples of the china, glass, silver and linen which will be used? There are all sorts of possibilities of improving on what we do at the moment.

Adam: Well perhaps we don't entirely know what we do at the moment. Still I am sure that our promotional material alone could be greatly improved. Brochures, room plans, sample menus; we really shouldn't stint on the production of these items, they are the backbone of our advertising and public relations effort. Without getting into a long discussion on advertising, I should say that direct mail is one of the most effective ways of obtaining banqueting sales. It stands to reason that promotional material should contain as much information as the client would require at any early stage and at the same time reflect the standards and image of the hotel.

Gaynor: Certainly but we know that direct mail may not be the complete answer. We have to consider a sales campaign as a whole, to what extent would we also want to use advertising and personal sales calls. All these have to be tied together and properly co-ordinated. For example, one could envisage an advertisement appearing in the local paper in the morning of the same day that our direct mail comes through the letter box and in the afternoon the salesman makes his personal call. It may not be that these should be as close together as this, but you see what I am getting at?

Adam: I certainly do. Yes, there's a lot of ground that needs covering.

Gaynor: Well let's start covering it. Now the other thing I mentioned earlier is the question of monitoring the profitability of a banqueting department. To do this properly other operating costs, apart from the cost of food and drink, must be separated and allocated to banqueting in order to arrive at a departmental profit or loss. It is no good saying that this is impossible and that nobody can say, for example, how much of the kitchen wages should be allocated to banqueting. Good heavens, even a guess is better than nothing. As for operating expenses, well I can't see any difficulty in allocating the cost of linen, glassware, cleaning supplies, ashtrays, menus and all these other things.

Adam: No, I think that it might take a little time but if one really looked into it, I am sure that we could find a fairly sound basis for the allocation of labour costs. Anyway this separation only involves the kitchen staff. Waiters, bar staff and cloakroom staff would all be quite straightforward. Why couldn't we just calculate a standard cost for the staffing of the kitchen to service the restaurants, floor service and so on? Then everything above this could be attributable to banqueting. As far as any overtime is concerned, the chef could indicate whether it was necessitated by banquets or extra business in the restaurants.

Gaynor: This is what I am asking for. Not to say that it can't be done long before anyone has thoroughly explored ways and means of doing it.

Adam: Well, where to now Mr. Gaynor?

Gaynor: I thought we could consider developing a questionnaire to ascertain exactly how things are done at present in each of our hotels. The sort of thing we could send out to each banqueting manager, together with his general manager, to complete. This would then give us an accurate idea of where we stand at present. Then we could hammer out some firm guidelines for each hotel to follow and hope to obtain managements commitment to an overall improvement. How does that sound?

Adam: Fine Mr. Gaynor. I'm delighted that you suggested a questionnaire of this sort. I think it's a format which would lend itself very well not only to the collecting of information about the current state of affairs, it also might provoke managers to start taking a more analytic approach to their operations. In fact, I once prepared something of this sort for housekeeping departments, perhaps I could show it to you sometime?

Gaynor: Yes Adam. I'd love to see it. Now how about that second glass of sherry.

Adam: Yes, I think I'm ready for it now.

6

A CASE OF NERVES

Happiness and progress go hand in hand, with happiness leading ... pain has its use as an indicator of missing the way and gives direction back into the path of happiness.

LIN YUTANG

Gaynor bustled down the office corridor in his characteristic manner, met Adam, greeted him with a brisk good morning, swept on and then came to a sudden halt. He had become conscious that Adam had given no acknowledgement to his greeting. He turned and called after him in a loud voice which caused Adam to jump and turn in Gaynor's direction.

Adam: Yes, Mr. Gaynor.

Gaynor: Adam what's the matter with you? Goodness, you're so pre-occupied these days that you go walking round in a dream. Do you realise, I said 'good morning' just now and walked right past you. You didn't even see me, let alone hear me. What's the matter with you—why don't you relax a little, you seem to be carrying all the worries of the world around?

Adam: I'm sorry, sir, I was pre-occupied with something on my mind. To tell you the truth I really am rather concerned, I have just been talking to young Jones, a trainee who works round the corner at the Isis Hotel. I don't know if you recall him, we took him on about a year ago straight from a technical college.

Gaynor: Yes I do, he is a young fair headed boy. What's the matter then?

Adam: Well, I know that people have not been very happy with him recently. He started off very well but lately he has been showing complete disinterest, arriving late, making mistakes of various sorts and so on. Anyway they can't do anything with him. Various people have talked to him, including the Isis Personnel Manager, and he just doesn't react. In the end, mainly I think because I was involved in his being given the job with us, they asked me to talk to him. I have just finished this minute.

Gaynor: Wait a minute, Adam, I have some time now, can we go into my office, make ourselves comfortable and tell me some more.

*

After reaching Gaynor's office, Adam continued:

Adam: Perhaps I am building the thing up to be more than it really is. It's just that Jones doesn't seem to be his normal self; quite honestly, I think he is on the verge of a nervous breakdown. He appears to be suffering from a sort of personality disintegration. I find it all very curious and it really worries me. I wish you could have heard our talk this afternoon!

Gaynor: What exactly did he say?

Adam: To start with we talked about his job and how he was getting on as assistant reception manager. He said that the department was under fearful pressure, that the staff were not able to perform their jobs properly because there weren't enough of them, and that there were all sorts of problems that nobody seemed to understand. He went on and on in this vein but whenever I questioned him, he couldn't really validate anything he said. In any case, I know fairly well that nearly all of it just isn't true. I know too that the Reception Manager and even the General Manager have shown a lot of interest in him and really tried to help him.

Gaynor: What then?

Adam: When I started to question him about the things I had heard such as lateness, his irresponsibility and some specific instances of negligence, he started to cry. He said he couldn't stand it any more and would just have to give up. He started to get into a terrible state of nerves and finished up, sitting there in front of me, with his head in his hands. I succeeded in calming him down a little and asked him if he was ill and whether he had seen a doctor to see if he had anything wrong with him.

Gaynor: Well he must have to behave like that. What did he say?

Adam: He said he hadn't felt well at all lately. He said that his stomach had been very upset, that he kept breaking out in a sweat, that he was getting intermittent palpitations of the heart, that he had pains in the back and so on. Anyway, it appears that he had seen his doctor who could find nothing wrong with him but had then sent him to a specialist with the same result. The doctor had told him that it was all nerves—he would have to relax—have a couple of weeks off—a complete rest—and snap out of it.

Gaynor: Did he have a couple of weeks off?

Adam: No, he had a week off but didn't feel the least bit better when he came back to work.

Gaynor: Well, if his doctor and a specialist said there was nothing wrong with him he had better pull himself together. We can't afford to waste a lot of time with temperamental young men who want to act the prima donna.

Adam: Well, I both agree and disagree with you and that's why this whole thing worries me. You see this is far from the first case that I have come across; in fact they appear to be all too numerous. People somehow experiencing tremendous tension and pressure and ceasing to behave as they would normally. This behaviour, you will note, is not at all typical of Jones; this boy is ambitious, keen, enthusiastic and, under ordinary circumstances, would be just the sort of trainee we want. Even the symptoms are all too familiar; I don't need to have any sort of medical knowledge, especially as he has seen his doctor, to conclude that it is a straightforward case of nerves. But what frightens me is that a doctor should turn him out with a week off and an exhortation to snap out of it! I would think that must introduce all sorts of further anxiety and make him even worse. I mean, if a person has psychogenic symptoms then he can't really have any conscious control over the way he feels. He needs help. That's the pity—he doesn't get help from anybody. All he gets are platitudes, recriminations and perhaps some pills. Worst of all, what we tend to do is to warn somebody in this sort of state to improve their job performance and when they don't, we eventually fire them. Can you imagine what that must do on top of everything else, a further crisis of confidence and the further anxiety it must bring on? Although they might have recovered, it becomes too late, and *we* must have pushed them into a complete breakdown.

Gaynor: But what's the world coming to, Adam? We didn't have all this nervous nonsense when I was young. I don't know what we're supposed to do—we are in the hotel business! We are not doctors or psychologists. On the contrary, we are completely ignorant of these things and we would be quite wrong to meddle with them.

Adam: I couldn't agree with you more, Mr. Gaynor, we would be wrong to meddle with them. I, for one, am very conscious of my ignorance in these matters and I am certainly not going to try and play amateur doctor or psychologist. I do claim, however, that I can perceive the symptoms and that I diagnose what is, in all probability and in very broad terms, a serious nervous condition. I will have no idea and will not try to ascertain how it came about and why since that is not my job. On the other hand, I must be aware that it would be wrong to adopt an approach of warning and threatening the man to pull himself together. I cannot judge him by normal criteria and, as a result, finish up by firing him. It's all very well to say that we don't want to be bothered by nervous cases like this but we may be losing what are otherwise first class employees. After all it may be one of us next.

Gaynor: Oh no, certainly not me Adam, I am as stable as they come! My ulcer is from too much gin and french and pipe tobacco, not from nerves. You too Adam. Good heavens, I have never seen you excited in your life.

Adam: Well, who knows about the future, I think that's the point? These things can often take us as much by surprise as other people. This brings us to your earlier point when you asked 'why'? I would certainly find it very difficult to answer that but I suppose it must be something to do with the stresses and strains of modern life. What is expected of people and what they have to cope with has become so much more demanding and generates far more pressure for them to withstand. Values associated with success have become more exacting, education is more demanding and more must be conquered both at school and university. The availability of credit in a modern consumer society tends to give people a continuing problem of debt to cope with. Add to these sorts of things the noise, bustle, long hours travelling—all the trappings of modern life—and it amounts to a very considerable strain. I think, too, that in the younger person entering industry for the first time there may be an effect of disillusionment. Most of them, I am sure, would deny that they are idealists, but nevertheless having to come to terms with their ideals and aspirations must generate some stress.

Gaynor: Yes, I suppose so. But all of the things you have mentioned are of a very material nature. Maybe it really is as much to do with the spiritual aspects of life. In the past there seemed to be a more simple life with a simple faith. People accepted institutionalised values, prayed to God and accepted the comfort given by Mother Church. The horrors of war were rationalised to them in simple terms, they were sheltered from an awareness of many of the tragic predicaments of their fellow humans such as the starvation, the injustice, the inhumanity. Things have now changed. There has been a rejection of institutionalised values and of the spiritual values of old. The increasing waves of secularism have left the Church floundering around to modernise her ideas and develop a new role and all of this may have had a shattering effect on many an individual life. Television, too, has brought the average person face to face with the terrible issues of the day, such as insurrection and localised warfare. I think many people have nothing to turn to any more. They have nothing by which they can come to terms with the tragedy of this world.

Adam: Well, you're speaking in very general terms but there maybe something in what you say. I think the 'why' question when somebody develops an acute state of nerves can only be answered for him personally and obviously that can only be done by a professional trained to deal with such a case. I am sure you are right, however, about the gap created from the fading away of traditional religion. There seems to be a frantic search to find something to put in its place—cults of various sorts, and so on. I even feel sometimes that people treat some of the new sensitivity and social skills training laboratories or T groups, which are used in industry, as a substitute for religion. They are treated sometimes with such fervour and reverence that they resemble revivalist meetings. Related to this I think that some organisational psychologists are quite the wrong people to come into contact with the types of nerous cases we have been talking about. They use criteria like emotional stability or the ability of standing up under pressure. If they show that a man can't, then they may make a recommendation against him whilst not realising that he might be helped to withstand all sorts of strain and pressure. In other words, they are not qualified to determine whether it is a permanent characteristic of the individual or just a temporary state of mind. There is the danger I think, organisational psychologists often don't know either. Some of them are just exhibitionists who are gambling in very dangerous ways with people's mental health.

Gaynor: That's a bit hard, Adam! I can see your point, but I don't think you should hit out them as a profession. A lot of people tinkering with sensitivity training are not psychologists anyway. You are absolutely right nevertheless in that this type of training has a part to play but should not be thought of as a panacea for all organisational and individual defects—or as a substitute for religion. I must say, however, that I have seen a number of these T groups trainers who have developed the demeanours of either high priests or evangelists. Still the use and abuses of sensitivity training are altogether another question. What we have in hand now is how to deal with severe cases of nerves when we are confronted with them in our own organisation. What do we do about your friend Jones? We are concerned with the timeliness of diagnosis to save the individual both for himself and for ourselves as an organisation. The analysis as to why he got into this state in the first place is not for us to pursue, unless it be something within our organisation which has created the stress and is the cause. In such a case we would have to locate and correct it before we have more people going the same way. What comes to mind here is that we might have some fearfully emotional and arbitrary styles of management which could conceivably create great stress for the people who were falling victims to them. I am sure that there are a number of managers around who, by their behaviour, are responsible for all sorts of ulcers, migraine and so on in other people. If we have any like this we should root them out. Anyway, we seem to be concerned with two things—counsel for the individual and counsel for ourselves as an organisation. How do we go about this?

Adam: What you have said has some frightening implications.

Supposing we have a man brought into a state of nerves by the gross inconsistencies of behaviour of the General Manager for whom he works. And supposing we are able to diagnose, by use of an outside resource, that the cause of his condition is due to the management style of that General Manager. Suppose also that the General Manager gets results and is a well motivated kind of individual who cannot appreciate the sort of stress he creates by his confused and inconsistent management.

Gaynor: Well, we would have to determine whether this case of nerves was going to be the rule or more the exception because of the particular nervous sensibilities of the man affected. If it were the exception we should try and re-habilitate the man and place him in what might seem to be a safer situation. If it was suspected as being the rule, we would either have to try and influence the General Manager to change, or get rid of him.

Adam: Yes, but where and how are we going to get the right sort of counsel to help us with this?

Gaynor: Well we would seem to be looking for some sort of combination of medical and organisational expertise; something I doubt if it exists at the moment in one individual. Since we have talked of the shortcomings that today's industrial psychologists would appear to have in this respect, perhaps we should convince the British Medical Association that we need a new brand of expert such as an industrial doctor or an industrial psychiatrist.

Adam: I am afraid that seems a little far fetched.

Gaynor: Nonsense, if you talk to the medical people closely involved with life insurance you will find that this is the general direction in which some of them are heading. Anyway, it would seem to me, right now, that it would be a very good idea to try and appoint to each of our hotels a doctor who is particularly interested in the treatment of nervous conditions and the effects of organisational life on physical and mental health. We could use such a doctor to refer the individual for help and also to counsel us as to what we might do to help bring him back to being a fully productive person. This same doctor might also give us clues as to organisational defects which we might have and these would then need to be followed up using our own expertise or organisational expertise from the outside. The personnel manager would have to be the man to act as the catalyst in all this. Do you agree with this as an approach?

Adam: Very much indeed! In fact, I think we may be pioneering with something vital to the status of the individual and the organisation in modern society.

Gaynor: Now what about young Jones?

Adam: Well, I think that I should talk to the personnel manager and see if there is any possibility of finding and appointing the right sort of doctor to that hotel—then have him see Jones as soon as possible.

Gaynor: Splendid, let me know how things turn out, I shall be very interested. And Adam, treat this with some urgency.

7

OPERATIONAL VIABILITY

Count what is Countable—
Measure what is Measurable—
and what is not Measurable—
Make Measurable.

GALILEO

Adam picked up the memorandum and report from Serendipity Property Co. which he had glanced through earlier in the day and he now thought about how he would deal with Gaynor's request.

He reflected that any analysis would tend to be biased by the particular specialisation of the reader; it could be regarded as a problem of investment—or as a marketing problem. He was aware of the consequences he had seen of such a blinkered approach. Business problems rarely arose as neat packages with a label; even an apparently simple problem ostensibly involving food and beverage control techniques had to be related to the attitudes, and possibly personalities, of those required eventually to operate the system.

A second consideration, Adam thought, must be to avoid obscuring the issue with details and see the total picture, like seeing how the pieces fit together in a jigsaw puzzle.

It would seem, then, that to look at the Aleph Hotel on the information provided three points had to be considered: specialisation, an interdisciplinary approach and finally integration.

Adam began to study the report.

*

MEMORANDUM

From   Charles Gaynor

Telephone Extension

To   Adam Smith

Date   19 May 1976

Attached is a copy of the details about the Aleph hotel from Serendipity Property which I mentioned earlier.

Would you, with some urgency, please let me have your comments and ideas as to:

    1 the major weaknesses of the operation

2 where these weaknesses offer realistic possibilities for rectification

3 other major opportunities for improvements

4 where the main priorities would lie for any plan of action by us

5 what the future likelihood is of achieving viability.

At this stage I would prefer that we do not visit the premises and, if possible, avoid asking for further information. I hope that you will attend the meeting with Serendipity when this is arranged.

C.G.

SERENDIPITY PROPERTY CO. LTD

GLYNFORD HOUSE
NUGGET LANE
LONDON E.C.5

17th May 1976

C Gaynor, Esq.,
Managing Director,
Gaynor Hotels Ltd.

Dear Mr. Gaynor,
Further to our preliminary discussion on the possibility of your undertaking the management of our Aleph Hotel. I am enclosing details of the operation, under the headings you suggested covering the years 1974 and 1975.

We have been concerned for some time about the financial results of the hotel and would now like to deal with the matter with some urgency. As we have stated, we are essentially a property company and we feel that the disappointing results of Aleph Hotel is probably due to our lack of experience in hotel operations.

We would like to exchange impressions with you at a meeting of our Board to be held at a mutually convenient date in the near future. Perhaps you would then feel able to discuss the possibility of agreeing some form of management contract to our mutual benefit. Should you wish to visit the premises in the intervening time, we would be glad to arrange this.

We look forward to receiving any comments you may have as well as your suggestions regarding a suitable date.
I am,

Yours sincerely,
C.P. Ice
Managing Director.

Confidential

ALEPH HOTEL, BATTLEMINSTER—ESSENTIAL INFORMATION

1 FINANCIAL STRUCTURE

The hotel was developed by Achilles Tendon Ltd. and is leased to Serendipity Properties Ltd. on a 50 year lease which has the following basis:

> £60,000 rent per annum—for the first two years
> £110,000 rent per annum—for the next eight years
> £70,000 rent per annum—for the next five years
> £50,000 rent per annum—for the next five years
> £30,000 rent per annum plus 30% of net profits thereafter

The lease agreement commenced on January 1st, 1973, when the hotel was opened by Serendipity Properties Ltd. as their first hotel venture.

The capital cost, land and construction exclusive of furniture and equipment, is estimated at £1,000,000. The Serendipity Properties Ltd. provided the furniture and equipment valued at £200,000 and this was done under a five year hire purchase agreement with a finance company.

2 PERSONNEL

2.1 Management

2.1.1 General Manager

The hotel is managed by George Brown formerly at the Delicia Hotel in the West end of London. The Delicia Hotel is an old established hotel of great tradition and outstanding standards. As is commonly known, it is virtually impossible to obtain accommodation there as its ninety bedrooms are nearly always occupied. Mr. Brown came to the Aleph Hotel after ten years of successful general management at the Delicia. Indeed, his services were especially solicited because of this very impressive background and he finally came with the very highest of recommendations.

2.1.2 Assistant managers

The two assistant managers have been selected by the general manager. They are young men both of whom have completed technical college training within the last five years.

2.1.3 Chief accountant

The chief accountant is again a young man. He is a chartered accountant and had no previous hotel experience other than six months spent working at a resort hotel in Bermuda.

2.2 Other staff

Little is known of the other members of the hotel staff. Some difficulty would seem to be experienced in retaining staff due to the rapidly expanding number of opportunities in manufacturing industry. The relevant figures have recently revealed that there has been 130% turnover of staff in the last year. In an attempt to tackle this problem the hotel, even though commencing operation three years ago with a comparatively high level of wages, has increased this by about 5% per annum.

It should be added that no living in accomodation, other than for the general manager and assistant managers, is provided.

3 AN OUTLINE OF THE HOTEL

3.1 Location

The hotel is situated in Battleminster, a town of great historical associations situated five miles from the sea. It is located between the industrial site and the town centre on the West bank of the river. More precisely, it may be considered adjacent to many of the local industries whilst it is a good mile to the commercial centre of the town.

The hotel is easily accessible from the North/South road bisecting the town and is visible to travellers on the road from about 400 yards away. The view from the bedrooms on the front side of the hotel is of the town, with the Abbey in the forefront, and is very attractive. The rear bedrooms, unfortunately, overlook a soap factory. A large site, hitherto wasteland, adjoining the hotel is also in the hands of Achilles Tendon Ltd. who are currently considering its best economic utilisation.

3.2 Facilities

The elevation of the hotel is an inverted T-shape. The restaurants, bar and public areas are located on the ground floor with the accomodation block rising a further five stories.

Facilities consist of:
  100 bedrooms
    20 bedrooms on each floor

  65 twinbedded and 35 singles
  1 restaurant with seating for 100
  1 bar with capacity for 50
  1 hotel lounge—40 by 50 feet with seating for 30
   parking for 45 cars.

3.3 Service

A standard of service exists of the type customarily offered in an hotel catering to a discriminating clientele. Room service is available to guests from 7 a.m. to 11 p.m.

3.4 Image

The hotel has sought to project itself as a place of subdued exclusivity consistent with the former associations of Battleminster. The impression gained is such as to suggest words like 'restrained', 'elegant', 'tasteful' and 'pleasing'.

3.5 Price

Prices are as follows:

Bedrooms:	double £12
	single £8
	excluding breakfast
Restaurant:	an average expenditure of £2 at lunch and £3 at dinner exclusive of beverages
Buttery:	an average expenditure of 50p at breakfast and lunch and £1.00 at dinner exclusive of beverages
Floor Service:	an average expenditure of 35p at breakfast, 75p at lunch and £2 at dinner exclusive of beverages

4 MARKETING DATA: BATTLEMINSTER

Battleminster appears to be a thriving centre with a variety of economic activity, and it was on this basis that the decision to operate an hotel was made.

4.1 Population

The population is at present 55,000; recent years have shown an estimated 2% annual increase and this is considered likely to continue. Age distribution is consistent with the national pattern.

4.2 Transport

4.2.1 Rail

There are good services from most parts of the country. The railway station is situated two miles from the hotel.

4.2.2 Road

As stated previously, the hotel is located in close proximity to the North/South road which carries a heavy volume of traffic, especially in summer, towards the resorts situated a few miles away on the coast.

4.2.3. Air

The nearest airport is some sixty miles away and is not serviced by any of the civil airlines.

4.3 Employment

Unemployment is 0.5%, well below the national average. The largest employers are:

    engineering and electrical goods
    textiles
    clothing and footwear
    other manufacturing industries
    construction
    distributive trades

No formal training facilities are available for hotel and catering staff; the nearest are at Tiddington Technical College, some thirty miles away.

4.4 Industrial

Some 40% of the town's working population is now employed in manufacturing industry. This approximates to some 12,000 employees.

Industries by size are:

    Less than 10 employed 48
    11 to   50 employed 76
    51 to 100 employed 16
    101 to 200 employed 10
    201 to 500 employed 10
    Over 500 employed 8

4.5 Educational

There are 31 private and public schools within 12 to 15 miles of Battleminster.

4.6 Shopping

Battleminster is the centre of a prosperous and increasingly populated area. Recognizing this, retail trades have developed branches rapidly and this is likely to continue.

4.7 Agriculture

Battleminster is something of an agricultural centre. A cattle market is held every Thursday and is attended by a large number of farmers. A number of agricultural engineers, tractor dealers and merchants are also located in the same vicinity. The market is approximately three miles from the hotel.

4.8 Social Life and entertainment

There exists in Battleminster a wide range of recreational facilities. Golf courses, tennis courts and so on cater to a wide taste in sporting activities and there is a good theatre together with four cinemas. That there is an active social life is indicated by the existence of 280 societies, clubs and organizations of varying types.

4.9 Historic and scenic attractions

With the Abbey, several old churches, a well kept museum, the Elizabethan high street and the town gates, Battleminster is rich in historic attractions. The surrounding countryside, descending steeply towards the sea, and soft and undulating inland, offers a series of unique and memorable vistas.

4.10 Battleminster as a tourist centre

There is no institutional promotion of Battleminster. Nevertheless it enjoys a great number of visitors usually stopping for a few hours en route to the various seaside resorts.

4.11 Competing Facilities

There are only three other hotels in the town which might be considered to be in the same class as the Aleph. These are the White Lion, the Brambledown and the Tudor Arms which have 15, 30 and 18 bedrooms respectively. About 75% of these bedrooms have a private bathroom. All three hotels are of the 'country inn' type; they are all long established, well known, and located close to the town centre.

It may be said that there exists a dearth of good eating establishments in Battleminster itself. However, within about 10 to 15 miles there are a variety of excellent restaurants to which many local residents drive in order to have dinner.

There are no function facilities in the town other than the Civic Hall and Hittlemans department store. The former can accommodate up to 500 for a dinner usually provided by one of two outside catering companies. Hittlemans has maximum seating capacity for 150.

5 NOTES ON THE INDIVIDUAL AREAS OF THE HOTEL

5.1 Bedrooms

All 100 bedrooms have private bathrooms attached. They are all about 300 sq feet in size including bathroom. Simply but tastefully furnished, they are all equipped with telephone, television and radio.

Business is better midweek than at weekends and better in the summer than in the winter. The average length of stay is just under two nights.

5.2 The Abbey Restaurant

As stated, the restaurant has seating for 100 people. It is situated beyond the bar to the left of the lobby on entering.

The decor has attempted to recapture an Edwardian atmosphere in recollection of the strong associations with royalty which Battleminster enjoyed at that time.

The menu is mainly 'a la carte' and consists of about 80 items most of which are drawn from the classical French cuisine. A table d'hote luncheon at £1.50 and a dinner at £2.25 are also featured. The manager has stated that it is on these latter two menus that he really makes his money.

We are informed that the restaurant serves an average of 300 covers per week for lunch and 800 covers per week for dinner.

The highest standards of service are maintained.

5.3 The Abbey Bar

The pleasant bar has a total capacity of about 50 with seating for 30. It is adjoining and forms part of the entrance to the restaurant. The bar would appear to be patronised mainly by restaurant customers and the average takings are in the region of £100 a day.

5.4 The Battleminster Buttery

The buttery only has seating for 32; there are 16 counter seats and 4 booths seating four. It has access directly from the street as well as from the hotel.

The menu is confined to light snacks, sandwiches, cakes, pastries, tea and coffee.

We are informed that the buttery is fairly busy at breakfast, so busy at lunch that people are turned away, and rather quiet in the afternoon and evening.

5.5 The Hotel Lounge

The lounge is a lovely spacious room to the right of the hotel lobby. It has a seating capacity for 30 which together with the hotel lobby creates a total casual seating capacity for 45. Although the lounge does not appear to be heavily utilised by guests, it is considered to be one of the finest assets of the hotel.

5.6 Room Service

Room service available from 7 a.m. to 11 p.m. offers specially designed menus for breakfast, lunch and dinner. However, at lunch and dinner these include the table d'hote menus offered in the restaurant. Room service does not appear to be utilised a great deal and serves on the average 25 breakfasts, 10 lunches and 10 dinners a day.

5.7 Other Services and facilities

There is a small newsagent's kiosk in the front lobby which also sells cigarettes and tobacco and tasteful souvenirs of Battleminster.

A laundry, dry cleaning and pressing service is available to guests, this work being subcontracted to the same company which undertakes the laundry for the hotel itself.

5.8 Parking

Parking places are available for 45 cars. Parking in neighbouring streets is unrestricted during the evening and at weekends, but heavily restricted during the working weekday.

Appendix 1

ALEPH HOTEL: STAFFING

CATEGORY	DEPARTMENTAL CLASSIFICATION	NUMBER
General manager	Administrative and General	1
Assistant managers	Administrative and General	2
Secretaries	Administrative and General	2
Chief accountant	Administrative and General	1
Accounts clerks	Administrative and General	3
Accounts secretary	Administrative and General	1
Front office cashiers	Rooms	4
Restaurant cashiers	Food and Beverage	5
Reception manager	Rooms	1
Receptionists	Rooms	6
Switchboard operators	Telephone	4

Hall porter	Rooms	1
Assistant porters	Rooms	4
Luggage porters	Rooms	4
Page boys	Rooms	3
Chief engineer	Heat, Light and Power	1
Engineering and Maintenance staff	Repairs and Maintenance	5
Head chef	Food and Beverage	1
Sous chef	Food and Beverage	1
Cooks	Food and Beverage	7
Stillroom maids	Food and Beverage	3
Kitchen porters	Food and Beverage	4
Head waiter	Food and Beverage	1
Waiters	Food and Beverage	10
Buttery supervisor	Food and Beverage	1
Counter Assistants	Food and Beverage	4
Waitresses	Food and Beverage	4
Room service head waiter	Food and Beverage	1
Room service waiters	Food and Beverage	4
Head barman	Food and Beverage	1
Barmen	Food and Beverage	3
Storeroom supervisor	Food and Beverage	1
Storeroom assistants	Food and Beverage	3
Head cellarman	Food and Beverage	1
Cellar assistants	Food and Beverage	2
Timekeepers	Administrative and General	3
Head housekeeper	Rooms	1
Assistant housekeepers	Rooms	2
Chambermaids	Rooms	16
Cleaners	Rooms	8
Night cleaner	Rooms	1
Linen room keeper	Rooms	1
Linen room assistants	Rooms	3
Cloakroom attendants	Rooms	4

TOTAL STAFFING	139

Appendix 2

ALEPH HOTEL: STATEMENT OF OPERATION

Explanatory notes

Beverage   includes all alcoholic beverage together with mineral waters and soft drinks

Payroll burden	includes holiday pay, employees meals, national insurance and related expenses
Guest supplies	includes all items supplied to guest rooms, e.g. blotters, stationery, magazines, newspapers, flowers, soap, toilet paper, needles and thread
Paper supplies	includes such items as waxed paper, ramequins, filter paper, chop frills, doylies, foil wrapping, paper napkins
Bar supplies	includes such items as food offered without charge, e.g. peanuts, crisps etc; corkscrews, spoons, squeezers, stoppers, swizzle sticks, book matches
Financial year	The financial year for the statement of operation attached is January to December

EXHIBIT A

MONTH OF DECEMBER 1975

Year to date 1974	Year to date 1975		December 1974	December 1975
190,500	194,416	ROOMS DEPARTMENT INCOME	11,694	10,556
		ROOMS DEPARTMENT EXPENSES		
72,920	77,592	Salaries and wages	6,300	6,740
18,100	24,200	Payroll Burden	1,510	2,100
10,826	11,478	Other rooms expense (Exhibit C, Schedule 2)	784	932
101,846	113,270	Total room expense	8,594	9,772
88,654	81,146	ROOMS DEPARTMENT PROFIT	3,100	784
61,914	52,902	FOOD & BEVERAGE PROFIT (Exhibit B)	5,514	3,148
570	620	TELEPHONE—NET	36	46
490	400	OTHER INCOME	34	24
151,628	135,068	GROSS OPERATING INCOME	8,684	4,002
		DEDUCTIONS FROM INCOME		
43,770	48,490	Admin. & General Expenses (Exhibit C, Schedule 3)	3,728	4,054
1,000	1,000	Advertising & Business Promotion	80	80
7,996	8,796	Heat, Light & Power (Exhibit C, Schedule 4)	948	1,052
7,574	7,900	Repairs, Maintenance	582	674
60,340	66,186	Total Deductions from Income	5,338	5,860
91,288	68,882	GROSS OPERATING PROFIT	3,346	1,858

Year to date 1974	Year to date 1975		December 1974	December 1975
		DEDUCTIONS FROM G.O.P.		
10,000	10,000	Rates	834	834
60,000	110,000	Rent	5,000	9,166
52,000	52,000	Hire Purchase—Equipment	4,332	4,332
122,000	172,000	Total Deductions	10,166	14,332
(30,712)	(103,118)	**PROFIT/LOSS BEFORE INCOME TAX**	(6,820)	(16,190)
		ROOM STATISTICS		
56%	58%	Occupancy	42%	38%
£9.40	£9.20	Average rate per room sold	£9.00	£9.00
£7.00	£7.20	Average rate per guest	£7.20	£7.20
33.0%	30.0%	Percentage of double occupancy	25%	24%
46.5%	39.7%	Rooms Department profit	27.4%	9.3%
		RATIO TO TOTAL REVENUE		
9.4%	10.9%	Administrative & General expenses	11.0%	12.3%
0.2%	0.2%	Advertising & Business promotion	0.2%	0.2%
1.7%	1.8%	Heat, Light and Power	2.7%	3.2%
1.6%	1.6%	Repairs and Maintenance	1.7%	2.0%
19.5%	14.2%	Gross Operating Profit	9.4%	(5.6%)
(6.5%)	(21.3%)	Profit/Loss before Income Taxes	(19.2%)	(49.0%)

EXHIBIT B: FOOD AND BEVERAGE OPERATION

MONTH OF DECEMBER 1975

Year to date 1974	Year to date 1975		December 1974	December 1975
£	£		£	£
		SALES		
199,660	210,760	Food	16,100	16,276
74,000	79,000	Beverage	7,800	6,200
273,660	289,760	Net Sales	23,900	22,476

Year to date 1974	Year to date 1975		December 1974	December 1975
£	£		£	£
		COST OF SALES		
79,464	87,040	Food	6,600	6,934
30,340	33,574	Beverage	3,158	2,666
109,804	120,614	Total Cost of Sales	9,758	9,600
163,856	169,146	GROSS PROFIT	14,142	12,876
		OPERATING EXPENSES		
70,224	75,156	Salaries and Wages	5,840	6,210
16,200	24,800	Payroll Burden	1,360	2,080
86,424	99,956	TOTAL	7,200	8,290
		OTHER EXPENSES		
720	580	Uniforms	60	82
2,200	2,420	Laundry	164	196
760	1,220	Linen	86	128
2,400	2,290	China and glassware	206	182
1,220	1,300	Cleaning Supplies	126	110
390	420	Guest Supplies	42	50
1,020	1,200	Office Supplies	94	102
550	620	Menus	76	54
22	10	Licences and Permits	8	6
190	20	Music and Entertainment	30	20
1,210	1,160	Paper Supplies	100	84
54	70	Bar Supplies	6	6
322	378	Utensils	62	24
1,280	1,420	Silverware	104	120
2,240	2,400	Kitchen Fuel	184	208
940	780	Miscellaneous	80	66
15,518	16,288	TOTAL	1,428	1,438
101,942	116,244	TOTAL OPERATING EXPENSES	8,628	9,728
61,914	52,902	DEPARTMENTAL PROFIT	5,514	3,148
		PERCENTAGES		
100.0	100.0	NET SALES	100.0	100.0
		Cost of Sales		
39.8	41.3	Food	41.0	42.6
41.0	42.5	Beverage	40.5	43.0
40.0	41.6	Total Cost of Sales	40.8	42.7
60.0	58.4	GROSS PROFIT	59.2	57.3

Year to date 1974	Year to date 1975		December 1974	December 1975
£	£		£	£
		Operating Expenses		
25.7	25.9	Salaries and Wages	24.4	27.6
6.0	8.6	Payroll Burden	5.7	9.3
5.7	5.6	Other Expenses	6.0	6.4
37.4	40.1	Total Expenses	36.1	43.3
22.6	18.3	DEPARTMENTAL PROFIT	23.1	14.0

EXHIBIT C

MONTH OF DECEMBER 1975

Year to date 1974	Year to date 1975		December 1974	December 1975
£	£		£	£
		SCHEDULE 1		
		SALARIES AND WAGES		
31,420	33,180	Front Hall	2,800	3,020
41,500	44,142	Housekeeping	3,500	3,720
72,920	77,592	Total Rooms	6,300	6,740
70,224	75,156	Food and Beverage	5,840	6,210
30,200	32,400	Admin. and General	2,480	2,634
—	—	Advertising & Business Promotion	—	—
3,000	3,000	Repairs & Maintenance	260	248
176,344	188,148	Total Salaries and Wages	14,880	15,832

		SCHEDULE 2		
		OTHER ROOMS DEPARTMENT EXPENSES		
320	420	Uniforms	30	42
6,200	6,500	Laundry	410	478
846	802	Linen	70	82
420	500	Cleaning Supplies	34	30
1,580	1,660	Guest Supplies	122	144
200	182	Commissions—Travel Agents	16	22
1,260	1,414	Miscellaneous	102	134
10,826	11,478	TOTAL	784	932

Year to date 1974	Year to date 1975		December 1974	December 1975
£	£		£	£
		SCHEDULE 3		
		ADMINISTRATIVE AND GENERAL EXPENSES		
30,200	32,400	Salaries and Wages	2,480	2,634
7,000	9,720	Payroll Burden	666	802
1,120	1,020	Office Supplies	82	106
580	620	Telephone and Postage	110	120
270	300	Dues and Subscriptions	—	10
2,200	2,200	Insurance	180	180
100	100	Bad Debt Provision	20	12
1,620	1,700	Legal and Audit Services	130	140
680	430	Miscellaneous	60	50
43,770	48,490	TOTAL	3,728	4,054
		SCHEDULE 4		
		HEAT, LIGHT AND POWER		
4,300	4,800	Electricity	450	520
286	258	Bulbs and Supplies	58	42
2,200	2,394	Fuel Oil	340	370
980	1,030	Water	80	90
230	314	Miscellaneous	20	30
7,996	8,796	TOTAL	948	1,052

8

MAINTAINING THE ENVIRONMENT

*A little neglect may breed mischief; for want of a
nail the shoe was lost; for want of a shoe the horse
was lost; and for want of a horse the rider was lost.*

BENJAMIN FRANKLIN

and for want of a horse a Kingdom was lost. Richard III

At a recent meeting between Gaynor and the general managers of
two of the company's hotels, at which Adam had been present, the
question of maintenance had come up. Gaynor had queried the cost
of maintenance and through this had probed the manning of the
maintenance activity in the hotels concerned. He had allowed the
matter to drop at the time but Adam could tell that he had not been
satisfied with the answers which he had been given. In fact later in
the day he had stopped Adam in the corridor and asked to be
reminded about maintenance because 'we must make a point of
discussing this a little more fully'. Adam had duly reminded him and
Gaynor had arranged that they talk together at two o'clock. At two
o'clock precisely Adam was ushered into Gaynor's office.

Gaynor: Ah, Adam, good. Well, I haven't anything prepared and I
haven't asked you to prepare anything either. You must have
guessed that I wasn't very satisfied with what I heard about
maintenance the other afternoon. I couldn't help feeling that this was
another vital area which we have rather neglected—that we've
rather allowed it to look after itself. So what I would like to do this
afternoon is just to talk around it a little; see if we can pin-point
what's involved; see if we can define what we are talking about;
examine where we've gone wrong in the past—if we have gone
wrong, and what we should be doing in the future.

Adam: Fine, as a matter of fact, knowing that we would be talking,
I have already given the matter some thought and looked into one or
two things.

Gaynor: Good, we might get more out of this afternoon than I had
anticipated. Well now it seems to me that with the very heavy capital
investment entailed with hotels in terms of buildings, plant and
equipment, maintenance should be one of our major priorities. Here
we are with hundreds of thousands of pounds already wrapped up in
fixed assets, with continuing capital expenditure every year, and we
look at them mainly, in rather detached terms, as entries in our

financial statements. What we read as depreciated values can have little relation to operating efficiency or the satisfaction of our customers. As far as maintenance costs themselves are concerned, we don't really know whether the amount spent is either too much or too little. Historical costs can be very misleading and, in this area, so can comparability between the various hotels because they differ so much in age and size and so on.

Adam: Yes, well I think much of this is true for all of industry and not just for hotels in particular. I would grant you though that investment in hotels is particularly capital intensive especially looking at the capital invested in relation to revenue. But it seems to me that what we must always be talking about concerns dichotomy of creation and maintenance. In our hotels we create, on the one hand, a production system and depending on the standard of our maintenance so will depend our ability to continue to produce. Of course, not only continuity of production will be involved but also quality standards and costs of production. Now I have hesitated to use the word environment instead of production system, but actually what we create is both of these things. It is also a working environment and as such will greatly affect the performance of the people in it as this relates to aspects of productivity associated with the concepts of a production system. After all the term 'environment' denotes the effect of the sum of external influences on an organism; in this case the worker. On the other hand, it is the customer because we create and maintain an environment which is actually part of what he buys. Whether he is using our restaurants or our accommodation, a large part of his experience will depend on his response to the environment. It is clear that having created the right environment and achieved the desired response, we must then maintain the environment in order to maintain that response.

Gaynor: Yes, interesting, Adam. It's really to do with stamina or staying power. It's no good if we are brilliantly creative if we cannot maintain what we create. If we allow it to decay and fall apart or if we allow it to become dulled and dirty, its first perfection is tarnished and destroyed. I suppose lack of maintenance has marked the end of many great civilizations, the ones that all fell finally into neglect and crumbeld away. The way in which a country maintains its physical environment could well reflect its resolution, determination and confidence in the pursuit of its national aspirations; in fact act as a reflection of its progress and its contribution to universal progress. The first symptoms of decadence and loss of dynamism might be rubbish littered streets, dirty or crumbling facades, filthy public toilets, broken-down public transort and so on. All these things could well indicate a lack of the necessary internal dynamism and a mood of stagnation. In fact, this is something that we could well call the 'maintenance' syndrome!

Adam: I think this is so true and of course it's equally applicable to hotels. There are many hotels which I have seen where the neglect and dirt both at the back and front of the house struck you immediately. This already tells you so much about the hotel without your needing to look any further. It's a safe bet that there is no innovation, just a negative approach characterised by an atmosphere of passivity and fatalism. Neither is it necessarily a question of lack of finance, even a poor man can keep his shoes shiney if he tries.

Gaynor: Well I am sure that our hotels are fairly spick and span; perhaps it's the attitude to machinery which I would be mainly concerned with. I mentioned public transport just now, well I am sure nobody would drive their own car until it broke down. Any sensible person would have it regularly serviced according to the schedule recommended by the manufacturer. Yet I wonder if we are as careful when it comes to the machinery and equipment used in our hotels?

Adam: I don't think we really know. The answer will entirely depend on the chief engineers in each of our hotels. Some are probably better than others and the standard of maintenance will relate to the calibre of the man in charge. I mean the engineer not the general manager; the manager may control the standard of general cleanliness but so long as there are no dramatic breakdowns or interruptions, I doubt whether he will question the standard of mechanical or electrical maintenance.

Gaynor: Well, I don't think that he would be able to, this is one aspect of hotel operation that most hotel managers are pretty ignorant about. I mean that a lot of the installations and machinery in a modern hotel are very technical and specialised. After all, this is why we have an engineering specialist in each of our hotels.

Adam: But perhaps this is just what we should be talking about today. You see these difficulties would be overcome if a system existed for both planning maintenance, and monitoring whether it had been done. Obviously, such a system would serve as a tool to enable managements to fulfil better their responsibilities. In essence, such a system would spell out what was to be maintained and when and how it was to be done. Reference to it in relation to the continuity of the operation would then reveal whether maintenance was effective. What we are talking about here is really threefold. Firstly, a recognition of the need for planned maintenance for continuity of operation and standards and for the planning and controlling of costs. Secondly, the criteria for developing the system itself; what type of plant or installation is it, what type of maintenance is required, what is the pressure and distribution of business to allow for maintenance to be carried out. Thirdly, what should the mechanics of the actual system be in terms of forms, procedures, methods, reports and so on.

Gaynor: Yes, I would particularly pick out your point about the type of plant or installation and type of maintenance. You see we are talking about the daily cleaning of a bedroom as well as the six monthly lubrication of a machine. Do you remember the approach you adopted with the 'Night cleaning at the Metropole'[1] problem; it started with work load analysis followed by work force analysis followed by job analysis. Couldn't it be the same here? What is to be maintained, and when and how, represents the work load, the work force analysis will concern the total staffing needed, and the job analysis will formalise the breaking down of the work into individual jobs and responsibilities.

Adam: I would agree, but there are two further points here. The first is how can you classify routine cleaning as maintenance because this confuses things from a point of view of departmental responsibility? Secondly, and this is very important, we may not be looking only to internal resources to cope with the total maintenance work load. In some instances it may be more advantageous for us to go outside and have maintenance contracts. In fact we are doing this already with some specialised items of equipment such as lifts.

Gaynor: Agreed, we should look much harder at contract maintenance as an alternative to home maintenance. After all, we do it with our typewriters. It might well be that it would be more economical and more suited to certain other aspects of the operation. I remember one hotel where we used to employ two full-time painters and there were 300 bedrooms. It took three days for one painter to do a room and each room needed painting about every two to three years. As a result of all this there was no alternative but to take rooms off when we could have let them. It stood to reason that we should get rid of our own painters and use a contractor. The contractor came in during the week or fortnight when occupancy was low and painted as many rooms as we wanted doing; he would just deploy as many of his men as were necessary. Whilst it appeared to be more expensive it was actually considerably cheaper when you took into account the revenue which had previously been lost. Of course, there were other savings apart from the painters' wages—inventory costs, space no longer needed and so on. Now this is only one instance and I think the same would apply in other areas, in one hotel we have a full-time television

[1] CS Chapter 3

maintenance man, in another we have an upholstery shop with two upholsterers; and what about the possibilities of contract cleaning? What I would like to see is a method developed to compare contract with home maintenance in all of these cases so that we come out with the right answer. Now, as for your point about the daily cleaning of rooms not being maintenance—well my boy, you've contradicted yourself! Just now you were talking about maintaining the environment to a given standard. If daily cleaning isn't doing just that then I don't know what is. To you maintenance still has this mechanical connotation. Cleaning is all part and parcel of the same thing. In the daily cleaning of a room you always expect the electrical and mechanical services to be checked; if there are faults then hopefully these would be rectified before the room was declared ready or finished. It's all concerned with bringing the room back to a given standard. Your idea of strict departmental responsibility is a bad concept in this respect. If a waiter walked across the front lobby and there was a discarded cigarette packet on the floor, wouldn't you expect him to pick it up? Keeping the place up to scratch, whatever the department, is everybody's responsibility; it's an attitude of mind which we should try and foster in all members of staff. In this respect the problem is, for example, the chambermaid who fails to report that a bulb is out because she thinks that it isn't her job. It *is* her job and it's our job to see that the system exists which will enable her to report it *rapidly* and enable somebody to attend to it *rapidly*.

Adam: Yes, I am sure you're right. But it's a vast subject that we're talking about.

Gaynor: Of course it is and it's the whole basis of running a successful operation. You said that you had looked into one or two things, what were they?

Adam: Well I went through some figures from the various hotels and there seemed some curious anomalies as far as some items of engineering supplies were concerned. Light bulbs, for example, some hotels seem to consume a colossal number. This leads me to believe that there is an urgent need for cost control. I mean it's strange that we should always be so concerned about controlling food supplies and yet completely neglect engineering supplies.

Gaynor: Yes, anything else?

Adam: Only that inventories of fixed assets are often not up to date. Thus new items of equipment are purchased but not properly recorded. You can guess that if this is so, the engineer almost certainly doesn't have a proper record of the item of equipment, its specification, and the maintenance either to be carried out on it or already carried out.

Gaynor: There is another aspect too: what one really wants in equipment is a minimum of necessary maintenance. This should be a criterion when we purchase anything or indeed when we design an installation. I think we could also refer to what I would term as 'designing out maintenance'; what I mean by this is identifying weaknesses that cause a great deal of maintenance. It is then up to us to see that such weaknesses are designed out either by ourselves or, whenever applicable, by referring the matter to the manufacturer. Another thing is that whilst we extol the virtues of planned maintenance on a regular basis, in some cases it might be that breakdown maintenance would be the better answer.

Adam: What do you mean exactly?

Gaynor: Well to take a piece of equipment out of service in order to overhaul it in a routine sort of way might seriously inconvenience the continuity of the operation. Thus one would have a duplicate standby piece of equipment to substitute when the one in service reached the point of breakdown or did actually break down.

Adam: I can see the advantage, one could then overhaul the withdrawn piece of equipment almost at leisure. Of course, another point is that it is ridiculous to go on spending a lot of money maintaining something when it is clearly worn out. In such a case it would probably be cheaper to replace it with a new item.

Gaynor: Oh yes, one must be careful in establishing very clear criteria here. Even as far as the total renovation of a hotel bedroom is concerned, the same considerations could apply. I'm sure it takes a great deal more time to attempt to bring back to a reasonable standard, on a daily basis, a worn, tarnished and threadbare room.

Adam: Yes, here would be a case of measuring the future cash outflows caused by excessive operating costs against a present cash expenditure for replacement. Anyway, in an extreme case it would be obvious that renovation was necessary in order to satisfy the customer.

Gaynor: Well, we certainly seem to have covered a number of points. Why don't you now go away and attempt to summarise what we've said? You could perhaps do this by attempting to list the maintenance management needs of the company. This would then serve as the basis for some sort of maintenance improvement programme. This should naturally embrace all aspects of maintenance and a system which could be employed in each of our hotels. Also, don't forget to highlight the training needs which would be involved.

Adam: All right, I think I can get something out quite quickly.

Gaynor: Good. Adam, please do that and let me have it by the beginning of next week. I don't think that there's much point in our continuing any more this afternoon.

Adam: Right, Mr. Gaynor, by the beginning of next week!

*

Adam had completed the summary decided upon with Mr Gaynor and had already sent it over to him as requested. It was as follows:

GAYNOR HOTEL COMPANY

A MAINTENANCE MANAGEMENT PROGRAMME

Part I Needs and Criteria for Developing a Total System

1 Needs
   1.1 Continuity of production and operation
   1.2 Continuity in environmental standards determined in accordance with the policy of the unit
      Working environment
      Customer environment
   1.3 Planning and control of costs in accordance with profit objectives

2 Criteria for developing the system
   2.1 Availability and accessibility of plant and equipment
   2.2 Type of plant
      Production areas
         installation, fittings
         items of equipment
         production standards
         environmental standards
      Customer areas
         furniture, fittings, etc.
         items of equipment
         production standards
         environmental standards
   2.3 Type and frequency of maintenance
      Mechanical and lubrication
      Electrical
      Cleaning

   Planned maintenance may be either preventive or corrective. The British Standards Institution define preventive maintenance as 'work directed to the prevention of failure of a facility'. They define corrective maintenance as 'work undertaken to restore a facility to an acceptable standard'.

Breakdown maintenance is defined by the British Standards Institution as 'work which is carried out after a failure, but for which advance provision has been made in the form of spares, materials, labour and equipment'.

2.4 Design feedback

'designing out' maintenance aimed at eliminating faults or defects which cause excessive maintenance requirements

2.5 Analysis of total maintenance work load

followed by analysis of maintenance resources

    Internal

        Housekeeping

        Engineering

    External

        Contractors

followed by job and contract analyses and allocation of maintenance work load

Part II Towards a system

Requirements fall into six main areas all of which should be considered and developed concurrently:

1 Maintenance/Replacement criteria

The criteria for replacement decision is indicated by an increase above the calculated upper limit in operating costs, and/or calculated lower level in operating efficiency

2 The elements of the maintenance system

2.1 Must allow for:

Inspection	Daily; Periodical
Reporting:	Daily; Periodical; Emergency
Maintenance action:	Daily; Periodical; Emergency
Checking:	Daily; Periodical

2.2 Hotel to be broken down into:

Areas:	e.g.	bedroom, restaurants, lounges, kitchens, stewarding, etc.
Sub areas:	e.g.	a bedroom, dishwashing area, staff dining room, etc.
Items:	e.g.	arm chair, burnishing machine, coffee machine

2.3 System to consist of:

- [ ] Sub area or item data and history file or card (normally a card for each item of heavy equipment but a file for each sub area such as a bedroom. The file or card will specify all details relating to item or sub area together with details of maintenance to be carried out or history of maintenance carried out. Details regarding renovation or replacement would also be included)
- [ ] Job procedures for carrying out daily or periodical maintenance and daily or periodical cleaning
  Work requests for the reporting of all observed defects or faults
- [ ] Inspection checklists for the daily or periodical checking of standards in an area, sub area or item
  (An assistant housekeeper's checklist for bedrooms would be designed to check cleanliness, require additional cleaning where necessary, ascertain mechanical and electrical faults and originate work requests. A plumber's checklist for periodical inspection of bedrooms may be designed not only to check all the plumbing but repair where necessary)
- [ ] Annual maintenance programme developed for a year and designed to show exactly what maintenance, periodical cleaning, renovation, and inspection are to be performed specifying when and where in the hotel. Programmes will be drawn up accordingly by area and sub area.

3 Supplies Control

Inventories of spare parts, other engineering supplies, and cleaning supplies, to be regularised. Purchasing, inventory control and issuing procedures to be established. Maximum and minimum inventory levels and re-order points to be established.

4 Techniques

The application of work study techniques to maximizing pro-productivity in all maintenance and cleaning work
Programming techniques to be applied for major works involving renovation or alterations

5 Training

Training programmes to be initiated in attitudes, skills and procedures.

6 Budgetary Control

Budgets of all maintenance costs, for labour, supplies and all replacement costs, to be developed as an integral part of the budgetary control system.

Standard costs for labour and supplies to be established and refined on a continuous basis.

*

Gaynor sent for Adam shortly after receiving the copy of the 'Maintenance Management Programme'. Gaynor smiled as Adam entered the office and waved him to sit down.

Gaynor: Good work, Adam, you seem to have arrived at a good synthesis of our discussion the other afternoon. However some of this summary comprises little more than headings, especially in Part II, so perhaps we can look into them a little further. My first point is about Part I though; here you mention this question of contract or home maintenance and you specify some of the considerations involved but you don't go any further. There appears to be no reference to it in Part II, now I think this needs stressing a little more.

Adam: Yes, it's true that Part II is directed mainly at the area of home maintenance. It's not that I have overlooked this question of contract maintenance but its full consideration would depend on developing an approach and method for making the choice. You yourself stressed the need for such a method. I believe that this is so important a factor that I would like time to work on it quite separately.

Gaynor: All right, why don't you take a specific example from one of the hotels sometime and work on it as an exercise? Now, my next comment concerns this question of availability and accessibility because this is going to seriously affect the distribution of the total maintenance work load. I mean how much of our equipment is in such constant service during the day that it can only be seen to at night? The other question here is what about accessibility to hotel bedrooms? The number of times that a maintenance man's time is wasted, because he can't get into an occupied bedroom, is very high.

Adam: Well, concerning bedrooms, the question of accessibility would become far less critical. If all the rooms are put on to a maintenance programme so that they are regularly checked and maintained, the number of times that the odd thing is required on a daily basis will be minimised. Here I would visualise a checklist for the plumbing, one for carpentry and woodwork, one for electrical services and so on. By planning in advance, liaison with Reception would be possible so as to ensure the availability of rooms for as little as half a day. This would allow for the checking and any maintenance to be carried out without, of course, losing revenue.

Now the same goes for items of heavy equipment and other installations. If planned maintenance is carried out then the likelihood of breakdowns and sudden crises is minimised. It is breakdowns which have no respect for the clock and happen at impossible times; with planning, availability and accessibility is possible during normal working hours. Of course, some things may best be done at night; lifts for example, if there is no surplus capacity, and certainly some cleaning. Even such cleaning as the main lobby might be arranged suitably for some very early hour in the morning.

Gaynor: Right, now this equipment data and history file is excellent in principle. Obviously it needs adapting according to whether one is using it for just an item of equipment as opposed to a bedroom, for instance. You have in fact mentioned this.

Adam: Yes, for a piece of equipment all technical data regarding specification and performance would be included. Then cross references to spare parts and the contact for specialist maintenance service or advice. Then details about the type and regularity of maintenance, these in turn would be cross referred to the job procedures.

One should also allow for the addition of notes on 'designing out' questions concerning weaknesses and faults. Data regarding rate of replacement of parts and relative costs can be included. Then the history of the item of equipment should be recorded, instances of breakdown or failure with the reason and action taken. This sort of information would be extracted mainly from work orders. This historical data would give a constant indication of how effective the planned maintenance was and would also give evidence for the establishment of maintenance/replacement criteria referred to. As I have specified, depending on whether one was dealing with an item of equipment or a sub area, either a card might suffice or an actual file in the form of a folder.

All requirements could of course be quite easily adapted to a sub area such as a bedroom. All furniture, fittings and installations would be included although a lot of data would clearly be kept centrally under the area file to avoid repetition. The history of each bedroom would represent the critical sub area data. It is evident that for a whole area such as bedrooms or a restaurant then a substantial file would be required. It would be possible as one refined a system to include more things, such as work study data, as to standard times for the completion of maintenance and cleaning tasks. All this would be supportive of establishing more accurate standard costs for both labour and supplies. Data concerning renovation such as re-decoration and painting, the life of furnishing fabrics, the life of light bulbs—all these could be successfully incorporated.

Gaynor: Fine, now about job procedures and work orders?

Adam: Well, I think I have already pointed out how they could fit in. But through planned maintenance one would hope that the number of work requests originated would be minimised. If this were done, the data would then, as I have said, be transferred to the history of the area, sub area or item. Job procedures clearly contain the detailed sequence for the carrying out of maintenance and cleaning. These, in turn, would be most important in training programmes.

Gaynor: And what about inspection checklists?

Adam: Yes, developed for areas, sub areas and items according to particular periods of time which would have to be determined. Thus one might have a daily checklist for cleaning whilst there might be a three monthly checklist for periodical cleaning. There might well be monthly, three monthly, six monthly checklists and so on for various types of maintenance. In most cases specific maintenance would be carried out at the same time as checking. In some cases, however, the completion of a checklist would result in the raising of work orders since the purpose of the checklist would be to check on the effectiveness of planned maintenance.

Gaynor: But you refer to the annual maintenance programme in relation to all of this. Surely this would be a very complicated document?

Adam: Not necessarily, one could have a separate programme drawn up by area and then a series of code numbers marked in according to date. These code numbers would represent either a checklist or a maintenance job procedure, cross referred of course to the equipment data and history file. It would be a very simple matter to transfer the information on to a weekly or monthly schedule for short term allocation of work.

Gaynor: Well it sounds fine in outline. There seems to be lots of details still to be sorted out.

Adam: Yes I know and I think that this is desirable. This is the system in outline and it can be refined and adapted to any particular hotel in any particular set of circumstances.

Gaynor: Well I think you would have to take one of our hotels which is fairly typical and then work a system out in detail, in fact design and tailor it for them. I think you even ought to go further and help them install it. That way we could have a model to demonstrate to the other units. It seems a bit pointless to think in terms of training programmes until you have reached this point. We certainly still have a long way to go.

Adam: With anything like this I think we are really talking in years and not months in terms of achieving something really sophisticated.

Gaynor: Well, the desirability of it certainly can't be disputed. I am so pleased too that you mentioned budgetary control at the end. As you say cost information can clearly be integrated into a budgetary control system and enable us to become more adept at evaluating and controlling the cost of the whole maintenance function.

Adam: Yes and not just maintenance either, we can also become much more discerning about design and purchasing decisions.

Gaynor: Agreed; by the way what are these programming techniques to be used on any major projects of alteration or renovation?

Adam: Network analyses—critical path analysis or programme evaluation and review technique.

Gaynor: Oh; well you'll have to tell me, or should I say explain them to me, some other time.

9

NEW FRONTIERS

*The primary function of art and thought is to
liberate the individual from the tyranny of his
culture in an environmental sense and to permit
him to stand beyond it in an autonomy of
perception and judgement*

LIONEL TRILLING

In the last week an issue had been raised by Gaynor which had
great appeal for Adam. The prospect of going into the continent of
Europe was what it involved. Gaynor had looked at two hotels, one
in Paris and one in Madrid, and he was seriously considering their
acquisition. It was early days yet and Adam had been told merely in
passing rather than in order to involve him directly. However,
Gaynor had said that he might eventually want him to conduct
detailed feasibility studies on both of the projects; in the meantime,
there was nothing he need do. Despite that, Adam had rushed off
and arranged evening tuition in French; there was nothing like
brushing up his knowledge of the language now so as to be ready
when the time came. His Spanish could wait for the moment
although Adam had made a resolution to work on that too. If we are
going to be an international company, he thought, then I should
become a little more international myself. So on this same evening,
whilst on the way back from two hours intensive French, he had
decided to stop at the Diana Hotel, which belonged to the company,
for a coffee and a sandwich. He hadn't been in the hotel for ten
minutes before George Kimble the manager spotted him. He came
bounding over.

Kimble: Adam, how nice to see you! Getting some more first hand
experience of the best hotel in the company I see!

Adam: You could say that, George.

Kimble: Well, you haven't been in much since that famous
Saturday when we whiled away half the day talking about ethics[1].

Adam: Perhaps it's because I find your conversation a little too
stimulating.

Kimble: Nonsense, if it was left to us we could sort this company
out in a week. By the way, what's all this I hear about old Gaynor
wanting to emulate Conrad Hilton and go international; the

[1] CS Chapter 7

continent of Europe first and who knows where else next? Come on Adam, fill me in on it.

Adam: It's no good asking me—I don't know anything. Why don't you ask Gaynor?

Kimble: Well, I've half a mind to. After all, I had five years over there with experience in France, Germany, Italy and Spain and I speak the appropriate four languages fluently too. I should think that I'm eminently qualified to head up a newly created continental division. What do you think?

Adam: Well, if you'd be serious for a moment, I might tell you what I really did think.

Kimble: All right, Adam, seriously then, what do you think?

Adam: Well, if it is decided to expand abroad and, of course I don't know that it is, I can't see that it need make very much difference to us as a company. The principles of hotel operation, or to go further, the principles of sound business administration, are the same everywhere. The only difference involves the question of language and there's no great difficulty in overcoming that. As to whether it's a good idea for us to have hotels in other European countries, then there's no doubt in my mind that we should. We could be in a far better position to exploit the bigger market for hotel facilities. With our marketing skills, backed by the right sales organization, this could be a tremendous step for us.

Kimble: Oh, Adam, you've more naivety than I gave you credit for! So language is the only difference? You haven't spent all your life working in this country have you? I thought that you spent some time in the States.

Adam: Yes, I was at University over there. But don't misunderstand me, I said the question of language was the only one deserving serious consideration.

Kimble: Come now, Adam. I can see that I'm going to have to tell you about some of the facts of life. I mean why do we refer to 'international hotelkeeping' as opposed to 'national hotelkeeping'. If we talk of it being 'international' then we must presume that some different considerations and basic differences exist when we look at hotelkeeping on an international scale. Now I admit that such differences may well depend on the particular viewpoint which is being taken. Firstly, there is the viewpoint which must be taken by an international company concerned with operating hotels in a number of different countries. Secondly, there is the very personal viewpoint of somebody completely involved by nature of being about to work in, or having worked in, another country. Thirdly, there is the detached viewpoint of people merely interested in looking beyond their own shores and horizons and seeing what the picture is elsewhere.

Adam: What a sterile and purposeless distinction. Why should there be any differences in international hotelkeeping—what's different about planning and operating an hotel here as oppsed to the States, or France or Greece or India or even Russia? Surely there is this universality in the principles and concepts of sound business administration or entrepreneurial decision making? Surely, techniques, methods and procedures of sound and proven use and application are of the same value whatever the country? Surely, the hotel market has the same characteristics everywhere? Surely the basic needs and wants of the hotel user, whatever the nationality, are the same?

Kimble: Well, you're asking a lot of questions, Adam. Go on. Go on.

Adam: All right, let's pause and have a look at the hotel market—this immense and growing chunk of people who use hotels. Let's say, and I've said this before[1], that we can segment them into four, these are upper income, upper/middle income, middle income and economy. Let us now say that each of these segments can be made up of some or all of the following types of customer; transient tourists, terminal tourists, residents and re-locating families, family visitors, institution and special events visitors, travelling businessmen, visiting executives, organised tours, convention and conference goers, and weekend escapists. Well, I think I could safely say that this would apply anywhere and everywhere. The only thing which could change are the proportions of types of customer who made up the total market and coming back to the concepts of segments, the relative size of each segment. Now in each and every hotel according to the specific mix of their market, what is offered for sale is shaped in such a fashion as to satisfy the maximum possible of identified needs. The market package is therefore developed accordingly. By market package, I mean the cluster of things which each customer buys and which basically consists of the location, facilities, service, price and image of the hotel. So what I am talking about are the absolute principles of identifying the needs of the market and creating a market package to satisfy them.

Kimble: Splendid, Adam, now perhaps we can glimpse a little daylight. The real questions of international differences follow your argument. Do the needs differ and in what way do they differ? Thus, in what way will the market package differ on an international scale? You have made no reference to economic and sociological differences in this. So let me now take these further and also relate them to the functions of management. These functions and the

[1] CS Chapter 9

approach adopted to them depend largely on the management style or management philosophy. So let me add another question—in what way does the management philosophy or approach to management differ on an international scale? Now I would sum up this little bit of preliminary thinking by saying that differences do exist and they are concerned with two distinct areas. Firstly, 'The Product': what is offered for sale, and secondly 'The Process': what is done to enable it to be offered. Now the answers that might be given lie in one word 'Culture'. One word with all that it entails—the canvas of a whole civilisation, different norms, laws, beliefs, habits, values, and all the rest of it. And you said that the only important difference was that of language!

Adam: Look, George, I've had a long day and I'm tired. Why do you always expect me to be on my sharpest intellectual mettle? All right, I was too hasty, but you know cultural differences can easily be overestimated in importance.

Kimble: All right, Adam, all right, but shall we explore this a little further or have you had enough?

Adam: No, not at all, carry on. Let's see if I can now contribute to this discussion a little more positively.

Kimble: Well, to carry on, in order to see the differences we are looking at three different groups of people and their behaviour. In connection with 'The Product' we are looking at the first group, customers and their needs. In connection with 'the Process' we are looking at the second group, staff and their management. The third group is owners and their expectations.

Adam: Fine, make a start on customers, the first group.

Kimble: Going back to your concepts of the segmentation of the hotel market and the various types of customers, I agree that these must also stand in the international context. Now let me add a simple psychological concept to this of two levels of needs, basic and acquired. Basic needs are those involving food, warmth, sex and so on; they are the physiological needs really, and obviously they don't change. Acquired needs are those induced by environmental influences and therefore they do change. However, the two levels often get confused, for example in the preference of a bidet in the performance of one's toilet. Anyway, the proposition which we must make is that if acquired needs are different from country to country then these will also be reflected in different needs as far as hotels are concerned. Now we can add a qualification to this because it is true to say that sharp national differences are being eroded away by a developing internationalism, particularly in the western world. The reasons for this are self evident and I don't need to go into them. However, the emergence of an international 'culture' is more likely to relate to the higher segments of the market than the lower. This is why we might expect the higher socio-economic groups to be more capable of adaptation abroad than the lower. Now going beyond this, what then are the differences which an hotel user will expect to see between countries? For example, an hotel in Paris may serve the same market segment and experience the same make-up of types of customers as an hotel in London. How then does the same customer's needs change, in the one-hour flight from London to Paris in terms of the market package offered? They won't change as far as location is concerned; he will still require convenience and accessibility related to the purpose and objective of his travel. To be near monuments and tourist attractions if he is involved in tourism, or industrial and commercial establishments if he is travelling for business. They won't change much as far as facilities are concerned; for instance, he will want the same standard of comfort in his bedroom and basically he must still be offered the same standard of service. He will also require the same sort of price levels in terms of expectations based on his home price mentality. Perhaps the key factor of the market package then is the image because this above all must meet expectations associated with the expression of the national character of the country. In London, he expects an atmosphere which evokes the very spirit of the city and of its role as the figurehead of the English civilisation. In Paris, he will want all those things, associated in his mind with both the city and the French civilisation, to be both pleasantly triggered into consciousness and to be further reinforced.

Adam: What you are saying is that an hotel must reflect, in the way that people see it, the civilisation, traditions and culture of the country in which it is located. I agree but I don't think that you have gone far enough in relating your concept of acquired needs as they relate to facilities and service. Depending on the market segment and type of customer served, some pronounced differences in acquired needs might exist. In such a case, an hotel should adapt its market package accordingly.

Kimble: Yes, each hotel should be conscious of this but let me relate what I said to the three different viewpoints which I mentioned before. You remember the first viewpoint was that of an international company; in each of their hotels they must observe the principle in order to satisfy both the customer coming from abroad and the local customer. For example, if a Hilton International Hotel did not convey the country in which it was located, it would alienate both the American tourist and the local people. In other words, the aim must be for its customers to enjoy the highest of international standards in facilities and service whilst still enjoying the particular 'flavour' of the country concerned. Now, the second viewpoint was of the person working abroad—the expatriate. For him the obvious value is in recognizing these things, and generalizing and validating on the basis of what he is able to observe. The third viewpoint, the person who is detached, well he can observe this by judging whether he himself is alienated by hotels operated in his own country by foreign operators. Enough of customers, let's move onto these other groups.

Adam: Before that, George, don't you think that much of what you have said also applies to operating hotels in different regions of the country? That regional differences, though not as important as national differences, still need to be considered?

Kimble: Definitely. For example, I certainly wouldn't call an hotel located in Liverpool 'The Londoner'.

Adam: Another thing is that a lot of what you have said is really to do with the sociological aspects of tourism and the general motivation of tourists. You know, I think this is a whole new area for work to be carried out as very little seems to have been done.

Kimble: Well you'd probably know that better than I would. Anyway, what of these other groups, staff and owners? How does the culture of a country influence the conception and operation of hotels? In the broad sense this is to do with the communal conditions of freedom; on the one hand, the way in which people view the exercise of personal or political liberty and, on the other hand, the way the government of the country restricts the exercise of personal or political liberty. It is, however, also to do with all sorts of other things which surround the whole cultural heritage: environmental influences, norms of behaviour, traditional ethics, religious influences, values and attitudes. All these change the activity of hotelkeeping from country to country. Indeed, as they change all other activities, so let me now take a quick step back to the first viewpoint I mentioned—that of the international company, and introduce a new concept—that of organisational change.

Adam: Ha, not new to me by any means.

Kimble: Don't worry, Adam, I think I picked the term up from you! Well, if the top management of a group or company of one country (one culture) are trying to introduce a management style or philosophy to a host country (another culture) in which they have subsidiaries, they are likely to have considerable forces against the change. At the same time they are not bound by the same limiting factors of tradition and culture, prevalent in the host country, in approaching the change. Indeed they are disseminating indirectly the culture of their own country in order to achieve a greater degree of conformity within the company. If the culture indirectly offered has positive, desirable and demonstrable benefits (such as higher wages or happier working conditions), then change is probably easier to achieve because the drive for it is not inhibited by the cynicism of those with greater insights into the culture of the host country. You know the people that say, 'You'll never do that in England,' or, 'You'll never do that in France.'

Adam: But this tends to start presuming that one culture is 'better' than another or would seem to be. This can't, of course, be true. I mean there could be no criteria on which to base such an assertion. Any view must be purely a subjective one based on an individual reaction to living or working in any one country.

Kimble: Well, supposing we were to use limited criteria of economic productivity and material well being, then there is evidence to support that the American culture is superior to our own.

Adam: You can't because if you were to, then one would have to say that an hotel operated under American management would be likely to be more efficient and more profitable.

Kimble: Why is this? What is there in the American culture which lends itself to efficient business performance?

Adam: I could make some propositions about this but they would be over-simplifying a very complex question. I would say that the Americans have preserved the democratic principle in society associated with the personal freedom of the individual. That is, they have maintained the communal conditions in which each white person is able to fully contribute to the society as a whole according to his or her talents. In other words it can be said to be an open society—dynamic, vigorous and creative. The cultural heritage encourages this and keeps the soil fertile for it to continue to grow. It flourishes and there would appear to be no forces which would either stifle or suffocate it. I could say that England by comparison is a bureaucracy which has stifled the flavour of democracy, out of a sort of administrative convenience and lethargy. Furthermore, I could add that it appears to have conditioned the people to the acceptance, rather than the questioning, of bureaucratic practice. The illusion of personal liberty exists but the cultural heritage has placed restrictions on the extent to which people would choose to use it. Its characteristics tend unfortunately to be conservatism, smugness and complacency. It is an orderly society.

Kimble: All you are doing now is to contrive little national caricatures full of half truths. Anyway, since it illustrates that national differences must be taken into account, let me continue with Spain. The Spaniard has never been able to differentiate between personal freedom and anarchy, and many times in his history he has been severely punished because of this. If I am Spanish and I am 'free' and you of a different political party, then I interpret 'free' as meaning that I can burn your meeting hall down. Perón once said in Argentina that he was anxious to preserve the personal liberty of citizens but only to the extent that it could not infringe on the mass of other personal liberties. This is the basic issue that the Spanish culture has always struggled with. Even Franco said that political parties must never be allowed to exist. The characteristics of Spain are volubility and passion contained within a stoic and oppressive fatality. It is a disciplined society.

Adam: Fine, well between us we have put forward a picture of the United States, England and Spain. What differences would these create in international hotelkeeping? What are the actual differences in the operation of an hotel in these countries?

Kimble: All right, let's have a go. What are the differences in the States.

Adam: Some fairly noticeable things come to mind I suppose. Generally there is an open, consultative and participative type of management. There is a chance for everyone to grow. Staff are encouraged to contribute to the shaping of the hotel as a whole—they are encouraged to be questioning and creative. There is little resistance to change and there is a general disposition to experimentation. Because of the tradition of the expression of personal liberty, people are more aggressive in manner. Thus customer/staff relationships have no basis in subservience, or sometimes unfortunately, even courtesy.

Now as far as England is concerned, some things also come to mind. Managements are generally not motivated up any ascending scale of improvement. Having attained, for example a certain level of profits they can become satisfied and complacent, seeking only to maintain the status quo. They are resistant to change. Staff, through years of being bludgeoned with bureaucratic controls, have tended to become passive, reconciled and unquestioning. They accept. However, whilst accepting there is often an underlying residue of frustration and they are quietly but bitterly and uncompromisingly antagonistic to authority. They are uncooperative. They will also resist change. This attitude is also carried over to customers because they are viewed as indirectly representing authority. Therefore one has courtesy on the surface but resentment underneath. Now what can you say about Spain?

Kimble: Well, organisations have a very autocratic structure. Management gives orders, staff obey to the letter and with a precision and diligence which is generally supposed to be Germanic. The onus is therefore completely on management to progress or regress or whatever. Of course, there are good and bad managements

but it is the manager alone who tends to make or break an hotel.
You see, the Spaniard will only respect those who, given the
opportunity, will choose to assert themselves over him. He reacts
well to a domineering approach but not at all well to an egalitarian
one. This of course reflects in customer/staff relationships. The
Spaniard also devalues life. Life is the enemy—life degrades
everything it touches. The feeling for life is essentially sensual, all
life is vital and vivid. The tragedy then is the proverbial rose that
wilts, the beautiful young men who must grow old. Life is to
blame—it eventually degrades and despoils everything that it
touches. Only his pride and honour enable him to transcend life's
tragic circumstances. His honour above all must never be
questioned, never be tarnished. The dignity which this imbues allows
him to withstand all that may befall.

Adam: Yes, but of course it is far too easy to dismiss a nationality
with a few words like this. We might just as well have said the
American is aggressive, the Englishman is passive and the Spaniard
obedient.

Kimble: I know, it's much more complex than this but don't forget
what we are doing. We are merely establishing that deep differences
do exist and that in the realm of international hotelkeeping we must
be aware of them. Now let's relate what we have said to the same
three viewpoints that I started off with. First the international
company: can it impose its culture on an hotel despite the host
culture of the country concerned? Yes, perhaps, if it attempts it
boldly and its culture has positive attributes which may offer
advantages and accrue material benefits. Indeed, there can be this
danger of being over conscious, and therefore over cautious, about
cultural differences.

Adam: And of course the market package must always reflect the
culture of the country in question. Your second viewpoint was of the
person working abroad. Leaving aside the question of learning or
developing in the area of specific hotel management skills, I would
say that there are obviously enormous benefits to be derived by the
sharpening of insights required when attempting to generalise about
another culture. Another advantage which would also arise from this
is curiously enough the sharpening of insights into one's own culture.

Kimble: I agree, for the person who is detached and uninvolved, this
can be a force against insularity. To look beyond one's own
frontiers, to view from afar but attempt to comprehend what is
happening in other places. This too must have a broadening and
beneficial effect when turning inwards again to re-look at one's own
situation.

Adam: Well perhaps I wanted to deny any real differences when we started talking so as I could get away quickly. George, I must be going, I've got a very early start tomorrow.

Kimble: All right, Adam, I've enjoyed it again. Goodnight and 'god bless the United States'.

Adam: Goodnight George and 'Viva España'.

Kimble: And Adam.

Adam: Yes

Kimble: 'Vive la différence'.

10

WHAT'S IN A NAME?

One day I wrote her name upon the strand,
But came the waves and washed it away:
Again, I wrote it with a second hand:
But came the tide, and made my pains his prey.
Vain Man, said she, that dost in vain assay,
A mortal thing so to immortalize
EDMUND SPENSER

When the conference on 'Marketing in the European Economic Community' had ended, Charles Gaynor looked around to see where Adam was. He felt stimulated by many of the ideas put forward by the speakers and wished to verbalise these to his assistant. Many of the ideas had been presented in relation to production and manufacturing industries. Gaynor wondered to what extent these could be translated into the operation of his hotel company. The main concept which provoked his thinking was the concept of 'brand identification'.

Not being able to locate Adam, he decided to call in to his office on the way home. On entering the building he encountered Adam.

*

Gaynor: Adam! I was looking for you at the end of the conference; I was so stimulated that I felt the need to discuss how some of the things which were said could be related to our own situation!

Adam: Sorry I missed you; I became involved with a number of people and we almost became a seminar of our own; but I picked up a great deal, both from the speakers and also from these informal contacts in other industries.

Gaynor: Why are you back here now?

Adam: Oh! I just wanted to check some things I had asked for on one of my investigations.

Gaynor: Will it wait?

Adam: You're my boss—what can I say?

Gaynor: To be serious Adam, while it is fresh in our minds, can we have a few words? Unless, of course you have an engagement for this evening!

Adam: Well, I did try, but she gave me the standard response of 'washing her hair' this evening, so I have no pressing engagements.

Gaynor: It's about time you got married! Still, I will avoid launching into sermons to bachelors; why not go to my office and see what we got out of the day at the conference?

Adam: That's fine with me, Mr. Gaynor, if you give me a few minutes just to check what messages may be on my desk.

*

A few minutes later Adam entered Gaynor's office.

Gaynor: Ah! There you are Adam. Anything on your desk of great importance to the Company?

Adam: No, Mr. Gaynor, just the usual trifles that I can sort out on the telephone tomorrow.

Gaynor: I sometimes think that we tend to get buried under paper when most things could be resolved by a quick telephone call.

Adam: True; but then you have your watch-dog Secretary and I spend little time in my office. Sometimes I feel that the only way that managers can make contact with Head Office is to write a Memo.

Gaynor: All right, Adam, you make your point. It sounds to me like another assignment for you! Still, to work: today's Conference. If you can bear it, I would like to express my views, but as I am sure you will understand, these are immediate reactions and will need a lot of later thinking.

Adam: Certainly, Mr. Gaynor, at the same time I would like to tell you of my reactions. I have recently been talking to George Kimble about the possibility of our going into Europe; doubtless my comments will be influenced by what he had to say, in addition to what I heard today.

Gaynor: Fine! Let me start off and then you can comment on my immediate reactions to this Seminar:

When you start to think about marketing, you are involved in a long-lasting effect. Once you make a decision in this area, at a top level, the consequences may not only be irreversible but we may be dead by the time they become effective.

Adam: If I can interrupt: while I agree with what you have said, isn't it most important to appreciate the intangible aspects—such as image—which involve both the customer and staff.

Gaynor: Yes, indeed, and on this point I feel there is no way of being sure of the 'right' outcome. The people who use our hotels must do it on the basis of their own life style or that of the companies they represent. Even if you engage in expensive market research, the interpretation and predictions still depend on an opinion—economic, social and psychological though the trends may be—and this opinion is associated with a high degree of uncertainty and risk.

Adam: Put in this light, it would seem that decisions are made in the realms of entrepreneurship; this not only involves the company in its responsibility for the company assets but also involves the highly complex area we describe as 'Company Objectives'.

Gaynor: As soon as somebody says 'Company Objectives', Adam, I always start to feel worried. Do you remember when you first started to learn algebra? All this hopping about brackets confused me—yet, with all modesty, I have become a reasonably successful businessman.

Adam: We could, at this point, start to discuss the relevance of the educational system to the reality of economic life—creation of wealth. But to come back to the main point: what has this to do with today's Seminar?

Gaynor: As soon as we start talking we seem to get involved in a whole series of issues—meanwhile the business goes on. Has it ever occurred to you that while we are away, attending conferences like this for example, the work still continues in our absence? We depend on a lot of people, who, if they suddenly left us, would be difficult to replace?

Adam: I agree, the faithful servants who have a loyalty to us and, in a funny way, are dedicated to their jobs. I sometimes think that we become too negative in our thinking—I mean the industry as a whole, not just Gaynor Hotels—by concentrating so much on problems of labour turnover. We ought to think more about problems of motivating people who stay with us!

Gaynor: You are, of course, right. Trouble with hoteliers is that when they start to talk to each other they always get bogged down in labour turnover, dishwashers, poor standards, etc. I know that you have inveigled me into attending this conference about marketing. Some of the seminars were rubbish—more like an evangelical meeting than a serious discussion of what we should do to increase our profitability—

Adam: And employee satisfaction.

Gaynor: Yes, of course. The thing that disturbed me about this conference is what they described as 'branding'. As you know, we have some negotiations going on at present to extend our operations into Europe. From what was said by some of the experts today, it would seem that there is an advantage in our adopting a 'brand image' if we are to extend into Europe. What do you think?

Adam: I must say that I was also impressed by what the speaker had to say. It also seemed to confirm some of the things we spoke about a little time ago.[1] But how do you see 'brand image' and how does this relate to us?

[1] CS: Chapter 10

Gaynor: It needs a little time, Adam, to digest the data we had today. I think I would need a little time to relate all this to our operation. Perhaps you could spend a few moments in preparing another of your summaries for me on this. And now it is getting late and I faithfully promised my wife to be home for some guests this evening; I thought we would have a few minutes chat as a result of the conference but we seem to have taken up much more time than I expected. One last point I would like you to consider, Adam, and that is our name. To what extent does 'Gaynor Hotels' mean anything to anybody? Of course we have our steady core of regulars who stay at the Zephyr and Metropole and other hotels; but do we have a 'brand image'?

*

MEMORANDUM

From	Adam Smith	Date	16 June 1976
To	Mr C Gaynor	Ref	10.21

Subject: Image and Brand Identity

1 We have previously attempted to examine what the constituents of the package may be when a customer chooses an hotel. It seemed that there were five factors involved: location, facilities, service, price and image. Of these, the first four are tangible, whereas 'image' is less so. Although the fifth can be described as intangible and is a composite of many things (letterheads, signs, uniforms, etc) the ultimate effect is the total idea.

2 This total idea is one which creates the total image of the hotel—and this usually occurs *before* the customer has experienced it. I am sure that you have seen rather seedy boarding houses sporting names such as 'The Ritz' or 'The Grand Hotel'. It follows that the name of the hotel, whether by tradition or cultural expectations, bears a direct relationship to the expectations of the customer.

3 You asked me if the name 'Gaynor Hotels' means anything to the customer. I think not, except for a very few of our regular customers. They mostly tend to identify with either the name of the particular hotel or with the manager or another member of staff.

4 The question then arises: to what extent do we have a 'brand

image'; the answer would seem to be that we have not. This then gives rise to the next question: *should* we have a 'brand image'. This must be examined in the light of any intentions we may have for expansion. This is particularly important to any intentions of expansion in Europe.

5 Arguments for 'Brand Image'

5.1 Many cases have been stated for an hotel uniform brand image. This hinges round the immediate association with a standard of quality and service, whatever the particular location may be. This has a great advantage in that the traveller, either business man or tourist, can retreat from what is an alien environment and feel safe and secure.

5.2 Referred business can also be enhanced, since the traveller can be reassured in advance that the sort of facilities and service he currently enjoys will be available at the next stop. In this context one has only to look at the record of Ritz, Statler, Hilton, and others.

5.3 Having a Brand Name also generates other advantages. The sales effort, for example can be centralised and linked with the particular needs of the potential client. Depending on the geographical distribution of units, purchasing can also be made more effective.

5.4 To some extent the Brand Name can provide a 'local protected experience'. By this I mean that the traveller can experience local traditional dishes in the restaurant while at the same time feel happy that normal hygienic standards prevail at the level he is used to at home.

6 Arguments against 'Brand Image'

6.1 The major premise against 'brand image' is that it devalues the quality of the product in the eyes of the customer. Probably as a result of higher levels of education and the influence of such media as colour supplements, TV, etc. there is an increasing exercise of discretion and search for individuality, uniqueness and exclusiveness. In our segment of the market, where discretionary income is highest, there is an increased trend in terms of original oil paintings, hand-made shoes, individually blended tobacco, and so on. In the retail trade, for example, there is a swing away from the branded product to the same product being sold under a private business label.

6.2 We are now a long way from 'economic man'; possessing an individual product is a demonstration of the affluence and success of the user. It would seem that as the individual achieves a perceived 'life style' the branded product is abandoned in favour of an individualistic one which reinforces this perception.

6.3 In recent times a move towards 'doing your own thing' has given emphasis and direction to individuality. A brand name seems to becoming associated with drabness, standardisation and uniformity; this leads to the discriminate individual experiencing a feeling of suffocation from the sameness of the package he purchases. Youth increasingly adopts an attitude of the importance of this individuality and an individual value system, and increasingly abandons the ready-made values and symbols of society. It must be remembered, that these are our customers of tomorrow. What is being rejected is the non-thinking, passive anonymity of the masses which result from the influence of modern techniques and persuasion.

7 Conclusion

It would seem a convincing argument that 'brand identification' is to be rejected at the level of the market with which we are concerned. This is the result of the perception of such as a symbol of conformity and anonymity. Ego needs are the assertion of self and the differentiation from the mass. It is the appeal of individuality which will develop increasingly over the next decade. It therefore follows that to think in terms of a national, or international, 'brand image' would be contrary to present trends.

*

A little time later Adam and Gaynor had been discussing a project and, since there was some time to spare, Gaynor decided to examine the arguments contained in Adam's memorandum:

Gaynor: Well, thank you for such a quick response to the question of whether we had a 'brand image'. I am not sure if your memorandum provides an explicit answer to this since you seem to have treated it as a wholly abstract phenomena.

Adam: I must admit, Mr. Gaynor, that I started out to try and provide a specific answer to your question. But I came to the conclusion that to do this would involve some detailed, and probably expensive, market research. I therefore concluded that it might be more productive to concentrate on the concept of the 'brand image' and see what conclusions may be drawn.

Gaynor: And you come down pretty heavily in favour of retaining the individual identity of units and avoiding any form of 'brand image'?

Adam: To some extent, that is true; but I hope that in my argument I have tried to be fairly objective and that the conclusion reached is reasonable, but still open to further discussion.

Gaynor: Yes, a good point, we could make it a part of the next meeting of our managers. How would you like to summarise, then, your study of this situation?

Adam: To try and do that is bound to sound a little pompous. Indeed, I am sure to sound like my lecturers at College. Still, Mr. Gaynor, it seems to me that modern society is tremendously complex and it is only too easy to over-simplify the interaction of social and economic influences. So, to try and summarise what I have said seems to involve four propostions—and, of course, again we would need some research to validate these.

Firstly, there seems to be an increasing search for individuality. It seems obvious that in the various socio-economic groupings there must be a relationship between the amount of discretionary income and the ability to buy individuality.

Gaynor: That sounds reasonable.

Adam: I would see a second proposition in that this individuality is a sign of affluence and a search will be made for unique products and services according to the buying power of the customer.

Gaynor: A question: if we are talking about our segment of the market, surely they are sufficiently conscious of us *as a company* and will tend to stay at a Gaynor Hotel because of a previous experience—or the opposite.

Adam: To some extent this is true, but then we have to consider who is the real purchaser? Is it really the businessman or his secretary; is it the tourist or the agency?

Gaynor: I see your point.

Adam: My next proposition is a rather round-about argument: even when the buying is minimal, the search for individuality is still being pursued. We have seen young people, for example, either buying second-hand clothes of another era, old army uniforms, and, with a common object such as a pair of jeans, adding colourful patches or appliqués. All of these seem to emphasize the need for this individuality.

Gaynor: That seems to be true. When I go shopping with my wife in the High Street I am frequently amazed at the variety of young people's dress. Yet, as you say, they seem to take something which is cheap from a multiple store, and make it their own.

Adam: I often wonder what would be the effect if you attended a Board Meeting in current trendy dress! The dark suit, white shirt and sober tie brigade would probably throw a fit. Not because of the success of your business operation, but because of the way you are dressed. . . .

Gaynor: Adam! I must admit that I sometimes follow a similar line of thought—suppose I attended a Board Meeting in the 'gear' (is that the word?) that I wear for gardening; but do go on.

Adam: My final proposition is that the brand name, or the brand image, is designed to appeal to a particular group of people. If you look at the tabloid newspapers, the sort of holiday package they offer is one of security. Sunshine of course, a stated price, an acquaintance with—but insulation from—the country to which they want to go. A brand name, I would contend, is appealing to the lower end of the market but not to our segment. And there, sir, I rest my case.

Gaynor: Thank you for your exposition. I now accept what you were attempting to achieve in your memorandum. But don't sit back and bask in the glory, because I may come back and want some more arguments to justify your case!

Adam: I think it would be appropriate to do this after we have had a seminar with the managers. After all, in spite of what *we* may think or say, they have to make the operation of a unit viable.

Gaynor: Now, in spite of your arguments, I still have a feeling that adopting a name which leads to 'brand identification' provides a guarantee of a uniformity of standards. In most cases, for example, you can be pretty sure that if you book into one of our hotels, you will have your own private bathroom.

Adam: That is very true of our regular clientele.

Gaynor: But surely, one of the main things about 'a branded image' is to ensure a uniformity of standard which is in accord with what the guest expects?

Adam: Again, sir, I have to say that this is all very well for our regular user. The thing that worries me about a number of different units who operate under the same name, is that the overall image tends to find the lowest level. I do not need to spell this out for particular instances which have occurred in this industry.

Gaynor: Well, of course, I am aware of this. But I do not see this as a problem of the image—more one of setting standards, supervision to see they are maintained and a control procedure that keeps head office informed of what is happening.

Adam: To a great extent, what you have said is what we are currently trying to do. But when we start to move towards attempting to decide whether we should adopt a 'one-name brand image', we will still be faced with two distinct aspects, which often get confused: what our future marketing operations are, and the interpretations which may be made of these. In the first part, we will be involved in what precisely the marketing opportunity is, if it exists, and to what extent it is defined by different people. Next, we will have to make a realistic appraisal about the Company's skills and resources to exploit the market—if we agree that, in fact, it exists.

Gaynor: I would have thought that we could do this by attempting to establish what our position is, as far as our market is concerned, its particular constituents and what market trends may influence these.

Adam: Such an approach must also involve us in what product and systems are needed to exploit the market of Gaynor Hotels. I think that we can see this clearly in a field such as an international reservation system. In some ways this brings us back to training; after completing the registration form, our receptionists must provide a follow-up along the lines: 'Your room is ready and you will find your luggage there when you arrive. May I ask if you have a reservation for your next stop? If we can help to arrange this, please let me know.'

Gaynor: I agree that whether one adopts a 'single brand image', or not, the product and system of operation must be with the position in the market, and so on. At the same time, I feel that we must not ignore lessons of the past. We must take this experience, examine it, and build upon it.

Adam: Past experience is very important, but in our subject of discussion, I think that we must also take into account of other people's experience in other companies. My impression is, that hotels which have developed individual names and personalities have been increasingly successful. Some of these have also developed on international reputation.

Gaynor: Somewhat rhetorical—but on what basis do you think they achieved this?

Adam: It may be that they provided what the market was looking for in terms of a superbly individualised product. Perhaps the less successful may be partly due to the brand name policy being ill thought out and poorly implemented.

Gaynor: The whole thing would be a very interesting study; as far as I know, little attention seems to have been given to this.

Adam: Yet again a situation where decisions have to be made with very little information available! In any case, it would need a group of companies representing different types of operation, to co-operate in exploring this.

Gaynor: One of the things which impresses me, from my travels, is that 'brand image' creates some guarantee of standards. This is very true from my experience in the United States, where I have visited a large number of hotels and various catering facilities which operate under a brand name. Some of these, of course, are operated on a franchise system, and there would seem to be some parallels in this country.

Adam: Since you raise it, Mr. Gaynor, it might be a good idea to explore the franchise system in relation to our own operation at some future date. There is an enormous appeal in this to the potential entrepreneur, for such things as small restaurant operations. There is also an appeal to the larger companies, outside the industry, who wish to diversify. As you say, it would be worth exploring. My major reaction is, how could we avoid the problems which arise, such as 'policing' to ensure conformity to set standards? Would you like me to look at this?

Gaynor: Not yet, Adam, let's try and concentrate on the issue of 'brand image' and the individualistic approach.

Adam: My turn, Mr. Gaynor!

Gaynor: Go ahead, Adam.

Adam: Suppose that we went for developing individualised hotels, which would project their own individual image: what consequences could we anticipate?

Gaynor: In some ways, I think we are already in this state. As you have said, a 'single brand image' needs well defined standards for the product and continuous policing to ensure conformity to these standards. Individualised units, against a general background of company policy, would require managers who could exercise a high degree of discretion. They would also have to impart their own particular personality as an important part of the image. Having said that, I must emphasise the importance of the general policy for the company to provide a general framework for activity.

Adam: This would imply a rather different approach, to the conventional one, in terms of the skills, knowledge, experience and personality in selecting general managers. While I tend to have been stating advantages of the individual brand image approach, we must also consider some of the drawbacks.

Gaynor: Such as?

Adam: There is a rather fine balance to be drawn in the exercise of discretion. For example, too much discretion in the area of sales could affect the whole company. It could also be dangerous to allow too much discretion about the product, since this must reflect, and be integrated with, the total efforts of the company. There may also be a danger that the projection of the individual personality may over-shadow the brand name. Finally, and this is a problem of building on the 'individual brand image', what happens when a general manager is promoted, moves or leaves the company?

Gaynor: These are, indeed, some of the problems which would have to be tackled in adopting an 'individual brand image'. We have, however, in recent times, seen a great growth in 'diversification'. Now I know that this is generally used to describe a major firm either taking over, or combining with another, in a different product field. Could we not think in a similar way of our Company diversifying into different areas of the market for accommodation?

Adam: I suppose it would be possible to soft-pedal the Company and promote the individualist image—at a greater cost, of course. We could group into various classes of hotels. So far, we have concentrated on the type of hotel operation which would appeal to the upper segment of the market. But rather than use the present crude descriptions, it would be necessary to adopt a more sophisticated approach. Perhaps it should be directed more at the social, cultural and recreational factors or the 'life style' of the consumer. At present, I think we can see a fairly well established life style of our customers and could even identify their profiles. Mixing market segmentations would lead to a greater complexity in this.

Gaynor: That would mean the analysis of each unit of the Company. And that would require different strategies for each unit, too! But to some extent, this could be overcome through groupings of the units, and possibly, by the name. By doing this one could avoid the regular, who wants a high class of service, finishing up in a motel with a much more modified level of service.

Adam: With our existing hotels, for the most part, we do have a Greek connotation in our name. What you are suggesting, is that, if we decided to operate motels a different and distinctive name link could be adopted?

Gaynor: A very tentative 'if'; please remember we are talking about *possibilities*! But I would see no difficulty of providing motels with names such as 'Gaynor M4 Motel', 'Gaynor M1 Motel', and so on.

Adam: Whilst keeping the Greek connotation as representative of our more luxury image?

Gaynor: Yes, something like that. It seems to me, from our discussion, that we have ranged over a narrow area without really looking at other broader aspects of the seminar we attended. Nevertheless it provided a trigger to some thinking. Picking up the points raised, both at the seminar and between us, we seem to be moving towards an 'all or nothing' situation. If we say 'all', then it means that we must adopt a name and uniformity, to which there are no exceptions. On the other hand, if we say 'nothing', it means that we must abandon a corporate image and present a personalised one to all our potential and regular customers.

Adam: There is also the possibility of operating different levels of service, and so on, to different segments of the market.

Gaynor: Yes, that also, but I must admit that I feel some discomfort in that concept. There is the old adage about 'cobbler, stick to your last'. I feel that the 'last' we have is the type of operation in the Company now. I am prepared to look for, and possibly adopt a new 'last'. But why throw away the knowledge and experience we have gained as a Company over many years?

Adam: Certainly, Mr. Gaynor, we would not wish to waste that.

Gaynor: I have just noticed the time! As my secretary has gone home there is nobody to remind me of important engagements. I promised to meet my wife at the Supermarket, with the car, and ferry home all the goodies.

Adam: Well, Mr. Gaynor, I hope that you will note the difference between the 'individualised' items and those with 'brand identification'!

Gaynor: I will, indeed; good night Adam.

11

COMMITMENT TO PEOPLE

Not only is there but one way of doing things rightly, but there is only one way of seeing them, and that is seeing the whole of them.

JOHN RUSKIN

Adam Smith walked down the corridor to Gaynor's office one afternoon for a discussion. Nothing very specific had been scheduled for the meeting, apart from some points which Adam wished to raise which were too minor to request a special meeting, but nevertheless should be checked out with Gaynor.

Gaynor's secretary was not in her office, so Adam knocked on Gaynor's door and was bidden to enter. He saw that Gaynor had been dictating to his secretary and just completed this as Adam entered.

Gaynor: Do come in and sit down, Adam. Miss Main, could you arrange for us to have some coffee, please? Well, what have we on the agenda for today?

Adam: I have only a couple of points, sir, which I would like to check out with you.

Gaynor: Fine, I have nothing special, so I would like to use our time talking about an idea I have. Can we deal with yours first?

Adam: The first is that Carson and I have completed the tests on the new detergent for plate-washing and, if properly used, could save us a lot of money. Shall I circulate our managers with a memo? I wouldn't like to distribute the full report, all they need to know is about the results.

Gaynor: Yes, I think you are right they don't want to spend all their time reading weighty reports—but I would like to have a copy. What do you mean by "if used properly"?

Adam: Well, we discovered that because of its strength, the real economies come from careful measurement of what is used.

Gaynor: Ah, I see; and that means that the plate men will have to be carefully instructed about this?

Adam: Yes, indeed. This is crucial.

Gaynor: And your next point?

Adam: It's about this credit card contract which has to be negotiated for the company as a whole. We should certainly get a better rate than the individual hotels have at present; it could be as low as two or three per cent, whereas the hotels are currently paying five.

Gaynor: Very good; go ahead on this, it should save us a lot of money. Anything else?

Adam: Not for the present, sir.

Gaynor: Good; Ah, here's our coffee. Thank you Miss Main. Well. Adam, tell me, would you regard yourself as a consistent individual?

Adam: Consistent in what way, sir?

Gaynor: I really mean consistent in your behaviour, your thinking, and so on.

Adam: Generally speaking, I think I am. But this is probably only true over a relatively short period. This is because one is constantly learning things and acquiring new knowledge which not only changes thinking and attitudes, but also affects our behaviour. So, I suppose, some of my behaviour would appear highly inconsistent if you looked at me now and what I did and said ten years ago.

Gaynor: Very interesting; and what do you think will happen as you get older?

Adam: Oh, I suppose that some of my attitudes will become frozen and I will tend to appear more consistent simply because I will rely more on experience than on integrating new learnings. I don't mean this will necessarily happen in such an extreme way, but to a greater or lesser degree I am bound to be affected.

Gaynor: So, that's what you think about us old codgers! But to be serious, looking at your behaviour on this longer-term, where would you say that you appear to be least consistent?

Adam: This is easy, in dealing with people.

Gaynor: Why do you say that?

Adam: Well, as a child one deals with grown-ups and peers in different ways. For the most part, adults have to be placated by conforming to the rules *they* have made. On the other hand, with other children, you can fight and quarrel or develop friendships and share secrets in accordance with rules, independently of adults. A similar situation exists during adolescence and it is not until mid-twenties that one really becomes an adult and accepts the rules of adult society. But even then, there is a lot of impatience with established order and a wish to get things done. Slowly one learns more about people and to appreciate their individuality and learn to look for their strong points rather than identify their weaknesses.

Gaynor: I think, of necessity, you are over-simplifying things, but I think I accept the main point of what you say. In fact, this is a process of developing social skills. As a young man I used to be very frightened of waiters; it wasn't really until I discovered that most of them had to suffer people who thought they knew more than the waiter, that I was able to appreciate how they could help me. If I showed enough interest in gaining and using their advice, they were interested in me. And it was not only for the tip, either.

Adam: Yes, indeed. A cab driver seems to be in a similar position. He engages in a large number of short-term contracts with people with whom there is never time or opportunity to establish any sort of relationship. Although it is a very broad generalisation, it seems that waiters and cab drivers respond most when asked for help.

Gaynor: To some extent this is true of most people. I have heard it said that if you collapsed on the pavement in London, people would step over you and say, 'Excuse me'. In Paris they would just step over you! But I am sure this is not true, at least for London! Coming back to my questions about consistency in behaviour, I wonder about consistency of behaviour in groups of people.

Adam: Do you mean the behaviour of people who belong to some form of social group?

Gaynor: No, from what I have read, members of such a group, providing that it exists for an appreciable time, develop their own rules or norms to which the individual members subscribe. Otherwise they may be punished or rejected by the group. If you take a professional group, such as doctors, they have a high degree of consistent behaviour in certain areas. We call this professional ethics and, if you are aware of this, you can predict what they will or will not do.

Adam: And in this case, you can relate this to the way they behave towards their patients or their clients.

Gaynor: Precisely Adam. Now if we take a group, such as our hotel managers, can you make predictions in a similar way?

Adam: Yes, I think so. From their training and experience they appreciate the importance of the customer and, within limits, treat them in a consistent way. In fact, this consistent treatment is probably one of our most valuable assets as a group, because the customer has a pretty good idea what to expect. On the one hand we are not going to embarrass the customer with scores of flunkeys, but on the other, he will be unobtrusively made comfortable and welcome.

Gaynor: I agree to that Adam, but you are confining yourself to only one half of the customers.

Adam: Sorry, I don't understand.

Gaynor: Well, wouldn't you regard our staff as being customers, too?

Adam: I see what you mean, we are 'selling' them satisfactions in working for us rather than for another company. And next, I feel, you are going to ask me about consistency in dealing with staff?

Gaynor: Right first time, you are becoming clairvoyant! I feel that in dealing with our customers, we have a high degree of consistency and I hope that we will continue in this way. Of course, I don't really know and I am only speculating, but do we also treat our staff in a consistent way? In the case of our managers, I am sure we do. But does the same apply to the treatment of staff *between* managers and between their heads of departments? I know that I have talked about this at various managers meetings, but normally in a very general way. In fact, I am becoming convinced that I have used so many banalities in this direction, I squirm with embarrassment! Now I remember your being somewhat resistent to written policy on another occasion, but would it help to create consistent treatment by providing some written guidance?

Adam: If I remember, sir, I was only trying to make a point that a written policy could give rise to bureaucratic behaviour in which people acted 'according to the book'. As long as one maintains a distinction between this and people taking decisions because of their commitment, I think a written personnel policy could act as a valuable guide. At the same time, there are now so many statutory requirements in industrial relations it could help to clarify the distinction between this and company attitudes.

Gaynor: We will soon have to start making plans for our next managers meeting and I thought this might provide a suitable theme. I am not sure that we could expect the managers to establish the policy there because of the time available. It did occur to me, though, that if we had a draft policy it would be a valuable exercise for them to work on this. Well, Adam, how would you feel about doing some of the initial work, we could then discuss it and later it could be worked over by the managers.

Adam: Very well, Mr. Gaynor, I expect to have some time next week and I could draw something up then.

Gaynor: Splendid, Adam. We can have a talk about it the following week.

Adam: There is just one thing Mr. Gaynor.

Gaynor: What's that, Adam?

Adam: I feel somewhat worried at the enormity of this task. Not just the attempt to draft a policy, but the implications of what may result from the managers' meeting. It may well lead to a statement which significantly changes our whole approach to business operation. That is, if it leads to a personal commitment and stance by our managers towards personnel.

Gaynor: It could, indeed; now you know what the drafters of the American Constitution must have felt like!

*

GAYNOR HOTELS LTD
MEMORANDUM

From Adam Smith   Date   7 July 1976

To   Mr C Gaynor, Managing Director   Ref   10.21

PERSONNEL POLICY

Introduction

The General Policy of a business enterprise is a statement of the corporate attitudes, beliefs and values which defines its purpose and indicates the goals which are to be achieved.

Within the General Policy, several sections can be identified which relate to Marketing, Operating, Finance, Research and Personnel. It is the intention of this memorandum to analyse the area covered by personnel Policy as a basis for discussion.

The purpose of developing a Personnel Policy, which is accepted and implemented throughout the compnay, is to reach a state of consistent treatment of employees in whatever part of the group they may be employed.

Advantages of a Specific Personnel Policy

1 The formulation of such a policy will provide a critical examination of corporate purpose and goals
2 An evaluation will be made of the values held by the company in relation to its employees
3 If made available in written form, the policy should lead to a clearer understanding of the company's philosophy
4 A Personnel Policy will develop a consistency in dealing with staff and so lead to better understanding of company goals
5 The corporate image can be enhanced both for the members of the company and for those outside, since the company is committed to a statement of its obligations and attitudes

Draft Policy

Some confusion exists between the following: policy, procedures, and rules. For this reason the following distinctions are made:

Policy: an expression of corporate beliefs which act as a guide to behaviour and decision-taking

Procedures: formal arrangements designed to facilitate the achievement of goals expressed in policies

Rules: prescriptions to act in a specific way (often with penalties involved for non-compliance)

In this memorandum the emphasis is placed on identifying areas in which a policy needs to be spelled out to achieve consistency. The procedures which may be developed from this will vary according to the unit in which they are to be applied, as well as other particular circumstances.

1 Recruitment

1.1 sources of recruitment preferred

1.2 vehicles for recruitment at different organizational levels

2 Selection

2.1 selection procedures to be followed

2.2 selection methods

2.3 recognition of formal qualifications

3 Wage and Salary Administration

3.1 rates of pay

3.2 merit and length of service awards

3.3 incentives, bonuses, profit-sharing, share of service charge

3.4 holiday schemes

3.5 wage and salary reviews

4 Training, Development and Promotion

4.1 induction procedures

4.2 availability of training

4.3 personal development and appraisal

4.4 internal promotion

5 Employee Representation and Maintenance

5.1 trades unions

5.2 consultation

5.3 dealing with grievances

5.4 suggestion schemes

5.5 employee welfare

5.6 health and safety

6 Termination of Employment

6.1 reduction of staff and redundancy

6.2 early retirement

6.3 discipline

6.4 dismissal

*

A few days after Adam had sent this memorandum to Gaynor, Gaynor came to see Adam in his office.

Gaynor: Shall I start? Well, I must tell you that I was a bit disappointed when I first read it because it didn't seem to give me the answers that I was looking for. However, now I think I see what you were doing: you want to keep it wide open for discussion and avoid giving too much away. Am I right?

Adam: Yes indeed, Sir. I struggled with this for some time and each draft failed to be what I wanted. Either I got involved with procedural details or I found myself making personal statements about what *I* believed we ought to do. I finally came to the conclusion that since this is intended to be a basis of discussion to explore and agree our collective attitude, the most that could be done would be to present a number of areas in the way I have. We can then look at these and try to find an answer to the question, 'What attitude do we have to this?' I think it is only in this way that we can achieve a degree of polarity among the managers.

Gaynor: Fine. That's just what I thought. Now I would like to discuss some of these points you have raised in order to clarify my thinking. The more I think about some of the headings, the more conscious I am that we have never considered them as a company before.

Adam: Well, sir, in preparing the memorandum I had the same experience. I find several gaps in my philosophy, if you like, about the employment of personnel.

Gaynor: Good, so we are not necessarily looking for conclusions but simply exploring implications and possibilities. Well now, tell me why you chose these particular headings.

Adam: I first had a look at what was available in the literature on personnel policy but found that this was not very helpful. Funnily enough the two that were of most use were relatively old. In the write-up of the Hawthorne experiments[1] there is the Employee Relations Policy of the company, as a footnote, which the employees used to refer to as 'The Ten Commandments'. The other example I found was by Northcott[2] who used to be Labour Manager for Rowntrees. Not only does he give some good examples but he is particularly clear in his distinction between policies, procedures and rules. And that is where most of the confusion lies. Eventually I concluded that the most logical way of building a Personnel Policy would be to consider the steps involved from the first stage of actually recruiting somebody to the final stage where he leaves the employ of the company.

Gaynor: That makes sense. Just two points, why do you place

[1] Roethlisberger, F. J. and Dickson, W. J., *Management and the Worker*, John Wiley Science Editions, 1964, pp 7–8

[2] Northcott, C. H., *Personnel Management*, Pitman, 3rd ed. 1955, pp 49ff

'Wage and Salary Administration' before 'Training, Development and Promotion'. I would have thought that it would be the other way round, or even that wages should be part of maintenance.

Adam: I could argue that agreements are made about wage and salary payments on engagement and should therefore follow selection. But I am prepared to accept that the sequence could be changed. However, I think that the whole area of wage and salary payments is so important that they should be considered as a group by themselves.

Gaynor: All right; my second point is on research. I would have thought that a personnel policy should include some statement about research, such as the validation of selection procedures or collecting information about comparability of wages with those prescribed by government policies.

Adam: This is a difficult one; I agree that there should be a policy about personnel research, but I thought that this would properly belong in the policy for research in general. Otherwise we start to fragment a research policy which should stand by itself.

Gaynor: Would you agree, Adam, that in the absence of an established policy for research, it should currently be included in personnel policy. Perhaps when we prescribe our research policy it could then be integrated with that?

Adam: Yes, that seems a reasonable approach. I hadn't thought of it this way before and it provides an interesting insight on policy formulation: as it gets more sophisticated, sections can be reshuffled to form a more logical classification.

Gaynor: It did occur to me that there are some analogies with accounting procedures in this. The small firm can get by with a relatively simple system which will provide all the information it needs. As it grows, more advanced forms are needed to provide information on cash flows and so on, and also for more complex decisions which have to be made.

Adam: I think the analogy is a good one and we ought to use it at the managers meeting.

Gaynor: A good idea! Well shall we go through these sections in sequence, I think some of them need to be expanded? Let's take recruitment, to start with.

Adam: First, I must say that in each section we will probably have to explore the headings given in relation to different levels of organization. Sources for recruitment will vary a great deal; from our experience we may discover our best waiters have been sent to us by a particular agency. In a similar way, we may find that our best trainee managers have come from a particular educational institution. In the latter case—and this is probably procedural—we may decide to adopt a practice of 'head-hunting' on an annual visit to the particular college.

Gaynor: I see what you mean, but there can be dangers of concentrating on one source so some flexibility has to be built into it. Now on selection, what is the difference between 'procedures' and 'methods'?

Adam: Selection methods are easiest to deal with first. We have to consider what sort of interviews might be appropriate. In some cases a departmental head may be sufficient, in other more senior appointments we might use panels. It is conceivable that we could adopt a 'principle of three', that is, the potential superior, the superior once-removed and the personnel officer or staff manager. This idea is based on the fact that anybody engaged has to work for a superior who must judge his technical competence; his boss once-removed is concerned with his potential for promotion; the personnel officer provides specialist advice on the appointment.

Gaynor: This is a very interesting idea.

Adam: I would also want to consider the use of tests in selection and this might properly be considered under procedures. I don't mean that the procedure for applying tests is given in the policy, but under what conditions psychological tests might be used. In a similar way, we may consider retaining a consultant to advise on appointments, particularly senior ones.

Gaynor: I think I see the difference, but it might be clarified by rephrasing. I like the point about formal qualifications, we tend to have been a bit lax about this so far. Mind you, I would be the last to say that because somebody has a piece of paper that we should employ them, there is much more to it than that. I also think that this should also be included in the wage and salary section. Something along the lines of financial recognition for qualifications obtained while working for us. For example, I have always thought that there existed some excellent courses for chefs who have completed their apprenticeship. We should *demonstrate* our belief with time off and, perhaps, a wage increment. I am intrigued that you should include rates of pay in the next section. Surely this is procedural?

Adam: I suppose that the basis of pay is affected by the relevant legislation, but we pay a great deal more than the minimum. Generally though, there are all sorts of variations which ought to be considered such as special rates for London or special rates for seasonal employment. There may be a better way of analysing this section but I think it starts with our attitude to rates of pay. At the same time we have to consider this section as a whole since wage structures will be affected by all the other things, such as distribution of service charge[1] and merit awards.

Gaynor: Yes, I see, but we will have to be more fundamental in our thinking about this; for example we should think about service charge, per se. If we decided that it should be abandoned, or rather incorporated in straight pricing we move out of the personnel field. What exactly do you mean by 'holiday schemes'?

Adam: Many firms operate a savings scheme for holidays and we could consider this, but with a particular slant of our own. Why not give special rates to our employees who stay in our hotels? Similarly, why not do this in association with additional days off with pay if annual holidays are taken in the off-season?

Gaynor: An intriguing idea—I never liked the thought of our employees paying out their savings to stay in other firms' hotels! It might be possible to make some arrangements with another company abroad. The training, development and promotion section is a difficult one; you can either keep it brief as it is, or go on for pages. I will temporarily settle for the short version. In your next section you have trades unions, but I am not aware that, apart from odd electricians and so on, we have any staff who belong to unions.

Adam: This may be so, sir, but it serves to emphasize the whole point of developing a policy. At present we have no unionization, but what would be our attitude if union recruiting drives were made in any area in which we had an hotel?

Gaynor: Ah, I see—forward thinking, I suppose we would call it! But do you think that we are likely to have any significant union activity? I am not saying that I oppose it, indeed there are certain advantages in having elected representatives to negotiate with. It's such a small-unit industry with so many transients that I would think it highly unlikely that an effective representation could be achieved.

Adam: I can't make my mind up about this. I was very impressed by the way the union was run in New York and it has overcome some of the problems. While it is true that they have a very different structure to British trade unions, they managed to keep track of frequent moves by using a punched card system. They also keep in contact with the Puerto Ricans through their weekly newspaper which has a section in Spanish. I keep thinking of our unions looking around for additional members and deciding that our industry, with over a million employees, would be a productive hunting ground. In some ways I think that our unions are an anachronism in that they originated in a different age and have not adapted themselves sufficiently to contemporary situations or

[1] Service charge is a percentage levied on customers' total bill, usually in lieu of tips, which is usually distributed to staff.

requirements. For one thing, we no longer have wicked capitalistic employers grinding the faces of the workers into the dust. If they tried it (if such employers still exist) they would soon have to close down due to lack of skilled workers who would have left to work next door. At least, this would happen in a period of high employment.

Gaynor: That may be so, Adam, but you would not deny people the right to associate for their own protection?

Adam: By no means, but it must be accepted that this applies also to managers and not just skilled staff. I would think it far more sensible for firms in a non-unionized industry to adopt a form of joint consultation at a domestic level. Our educational system concentrates now on people learning to be critical and our form of government becomes increasingly democratic. It is natural for industry to offer more participation and consultation in areas where the employees are going to be directly affected. Sorry, Mr. Gaynor, I should save this for the managers' meeting!

Gaynor: Not at all, Adam, I am very interested. I am afraid that, like a lot of people in this industry, I am not very well informed on joint consultation which I consider a form of trade unionism. To some extent the way some of our managers have staff meetings and discussion groups is probably a form of joint consultation. But I never considered formalizing this, believing it to be an individual decision by the manager of how he will conduct his hotel. One final point, Adam, why do we need a policy on redundancy when this is covered by legislation?

Adam: Well this again is a valuable exercise in formulating policy. The payments to be made under the Act are quite clearly stipulated. But if a group of people should become redundant because of mechanization or a change in policy in relation to centralization, what criteria should be followed? In manufacturing industries, where this happens more often, a policy of 'last in, first out' is often followed. I think there are better criteria which should be related to age, skills possessed and potential for re-training.

Gaynor: Thank you, but I will have to think about all this a great deal more. I have been feeling at some disadvantage as you have done your homework so thoroughly. Still, I am glad that we have started to explore this area; it just goes to show how much one can take for granted. I am sure it will make an excellent theme for the managers' meeting. Now, a practical aspect of personnel policy—our welfare. Let's go and have lunch, I feel we have done a good morning's work and ought to reward ourselves!

Adam: Thank you, sir.

12

ANOTHER CONVERSATION IN THE BAR

*No man can reveal to you aught but that which
already lies half asleep in the dawn of your
knowledge ... If he is indeed wise he does not bid
you enter the house of his wisdom, but rather leads
you to the threshold of your own mind.*

KAHLIL GIBRAN

Another week was coming to an end; late one Friday afternoon
Adam sat at his desk and savoured the week-end ahead. He had
arranged to go out for dinner that evening and was looking forward
to it with pleasurable anticipation. It occurred to him that it would
help to create a relaxed frame of mind if he stopped off for a
preliminary drink in the bar of the Isis Hotel.

Immediately on entering the bar Adam saw Gaynor sitting by
himself and walked across to join him.

Gaynor: Hello Adam, would you like to join me for a drink? I am
just waiting for my wife to join me.

Adam: Thank you, sir. I was just going to kill some time before
meeting a friend for dinner.

Gaynor: Two gin and french, John. Is that all right Adam?

Adam: Just what I needed, sir.

Gaynor: But I must say I am surprised at you Adam. Coming in
here to 'kill time' as you put it. What an objectionable way of
putting it! When you reach my stage of life, you start to think about
time a great deal; it seems to go so quickly.

Adam: The connotation never occurred to me before, it is a rather
unattractive phrase.

Gaynor: I wonder what we do with our time? There never seems to
be enough time to do everything. Every time I go to a conference or
read a book we are continually exhorted to devote more time to
thinking, planning, developing our managers, and so on. But where
are we expected to find this time they never say.

Adam: Well sir, some executives appoint personal assistants!

Gaynor: I take your point, Adam. If you take your job, since you
joined me I haven't really had any more time. You do a lot of things
that I *should* have done before, but never did because of the lack of
time. Now these things get done and we are better for it. So you see,
in my case having a personal assistant doesn't involve handing over

responsibilities so much as getting things done for which I never had opportunity before.

Adam: Perhaps there are really two aspects to this. On the one hand delegation is involved in which an executive hands over some responsibilities to a subordinate. In theory, at least, this should leave him free to take on additional responsibilities or spend more time on certain aspects of his work. On the other hand is the problem of how time is actually utilised by the executive.

Gaynor: I think you are right. I sometimes say in jest that my greatest problem is deciding what to do. And there is some truth in this. I don't mean that I have to look for something to do, but have to choose just what to give my attention to from the whole range of things with which I could occupy my time.

Adam: This is very like the problem I used to experience at college when we did cookery. There was no difficulty in preparing a single dish in a practice laboratory but you had later to do several dishes simultaneously in the kitchen. I found it very difficult to learn the programming for this, yet I have worked with chefs to whom it seemed a second nature.

Gaynor: Your analogy is very apt. I think managing is so like juggling. You have to keep several things in the air at the same time without dropping anything. If you don't allocate the appropriate time to each of the tasks you can easily get into trouble.

Adam: Yes I can see this; what you are really saying is that one dimension for evaluating executive performance is how successfully they do this time-sharing.

Gaynor: Oh, indeed! I think every senior executive develops this for himself. There are always subordinates who produce on time; there are others who need a reminder, and there are those who are always behind for whom you have to make allowances.

Adam: Yet if this time-sharing is so important, it seems funny that nobody seems to have explored it. I can't recollect any courses being held for it.

Gaynor: Well, I am not surprised. How could you teach it on a course? I would think that it is an integral part of on-the-job training that can only be learnt in operational situations.

Adam: I agree, but surely some sort of analysis should be made of managers jobs before this could be properly done! It is quite striking that among all the piles of literature produced about management most of it seems to be in the form of exhortation about what managers should do. I would think it appropriate to first find out what in fact they do.

Gaynor: But you must agree that we already know a great deal about what managers do. They have to plan, they have to deal with other people, and so on. These things are self evident and indicate basic knowledge and techniques they must acquire.

Adam: Oh I agree. One can argue that these activities can be observed and also acquired from personal experience. But I sometimes worry about the generalizations and assumptions which are made. I think it is generally held that managers are decision-takers but this really tells us nothing until we examine the sorts of decisions which they make. In one firm these may be far reaching and require sophisticated techniques. In another firm they may only be very minor.

Gaynor: There are sure to be variations in the importance of decisions both between firms and at different levels within a firm. But the process of decision-taking must have basic principles which can be examined.

Adam: That is probably true. I think that the existence of decision theory indicates that a rational process is involved which can be simulated mathematically.

Gaynor: I have seen some of this and I must admit that I begin to wonder however we cope with making decisions—it looks so complicated! One thing I can never understand though, is the assumption that an executive sits down and says 'I am going to make a decision'. In my experience it rarely happens like that. I may do all the things that they say, like collecting all the facts. But I generally mull these over in my mind, with important decisions, and may actually make the decision when I am shaving. With minor decisions, when these are brought to my attention, I use my knowledge and experience to quickly dispose of them. Now if you say we should know more about what managers in fact do, how on earth could you study decision-taking?

Adam: I am afraid I don't know; I know that some attempts have been made to do this and, in one case, a wide variation was observed between what a manager regarded as orders or decisions and what his subordinates took to be advice. But I would be less ambitious than this and would be happy with some simple information about what parts of their total job takes most time; what sort of interactions they have with other people, and so on. You see, so much is said about management development and training without enough being said about what managers are to be developed or trained for.

Gaynor: I am glad you introduced management development because I must confess to some uneasy feelings about this myself recently.

Adam: In what way, sir?

Gaynor: It is difficult to say, really. We hear a lot about management development, but it all seems too pat to me. I have heard senior executives using the phrase but the feeling I had was that they wanted to train or develop their managers to be like themselves. A mirror to them!

Adam: To produce organisation men! Well perhaps we all suffer from this tendency to a greater or lesser degree, just as a father may be disappointed that his son does not want to follow his profession. I think that the whole area of management development is exceedingly complex and must be directed towards maintaining existing managers and the learning needs of younger people to prepare them for senior jobs.

Gaynor: Well yes; I would have thought that this is an internal concern of the firm. After all it is only the individual firm that can know enough about the jobs its managers do and the goals of the enterprise. An external agency may be able to help by providing courses, but I fear that these may be rather generalised and I feel it is up to the firm to choose the right courses.

Adam: Perhaps too much reliance is placed on attending courses. One often hears of manager and potential managers attending numerous courses but never being asked to try and implement what they have learnt. It seems almost as though some firms salve their conscience about management development by detailing a number of managers to periodically attend courses.

Gaynor: What alternative would you propose?

Adam: I think it really starts with what we were talking about some time ago when we said management involved creating a certain type of environment. In other words, it is not just a programme written out for somebody about rotating his job or attending courses. It is part of the atmosphere of the enterprise where it is a matter of experience that those who run the firm *believe* in personal growth. We used the word 'ethos'.

Gaynor: I wouldn't disagree with that; however, there is still a high degree of involvement by the individual. After all he decides to join the firm to start with and he must decide that he wants to develop as an individual. To some extent this will be determined by his career objectives; if he sees himself stepping into my shoes he will be anxious to take advantage of every opportunity to acquire the right experience. On the other hand, if his interests centre round his garden he may well reject any opportunity to develop professionally if this were to involve moving home or working on a Sunday. I am also particularly conscious that in the early stages of his career, a manager has to contribute a great deal of effort and make personal sacrifices to achieve long range goals. It often seems unfortunate that this should occur at exactly the wrong time. Assistant banqueting managers always seem to be appointed in their early married life—just at the time when they want to be home in the evening!

Adam: So really when we talk about management development this involves both personal development and development as a professional manager?

Gaynor: I am not sure that they can be divorced in this way because I would think that personal development is an integral part of management development. The way I see it is that management involves three skills. Firstly are personal skills, such as using one's experience and judgement and learning from taking decisions. Then there are the social skills, such as are needed in relating to other people and learning the appropriate behaviour as a leader *and* as a group member. What I have called the technical skills can be misleading. I don't mean cooking or being able to carry six plates of soup. I mean the ability to apply technical knowledge about managing. One can know a great deal about accounting, but the real skill involved is to be able to look at an operating statement of an hotel and see the significance of the figures.

Adam: Management development is really concerned with developing these skills—I see. Putting it in this way can show the right perspective on management techniques. I have always been a little puzzled what is meant by management techniques. The phrase seems to be used in a variety of ways which can mean 'how to manage' or 'procedures used in managing'. I now can see that management techniques are really the underlying knowledge which is manifested in the technical skills. But having said this, it is still difficult to see how, in fact, the personal social and technical skills can be developed.

Gaynor: We are back to the environment again, I would see that developing personal and social skills essentially occurs on the job. But not just in doing the job. I believe the Americans talk about counselling to indicate a manager reviewing a subordinate's performance and advising him. I think that personal and social skills can best be developed by this counselling. Other means can help, of course; we have both had experiences, I think, of how one can improve personal and social skills by laboratory training.[1] However, in my own experience I have always found that I have grown as an individual when I have accomplished something different. It has always arisen from a job being done which to me was new, important and generally a complex piece of work. But to get the maximum benefit I have needed to know about my degree of success or failure.

Adam: You mean that managers can develop through their failures?

[1] See CS Chapter 8

Gaynor: Not if they fail all the time! But yes, we all make mistakes and, under suitable conditions, we can learn from these as much as from our successes. Now this is where the counselling comes in. I need somebody to appreciate successes and help to analyse the failures. Certainly I recollect that the people who have helped me most in my career have always had this ability to counsel me. Anybody in a management grade is bound to sometimes feel a little lonely and need some external comment. One tends to get too close to the job and never be quite sure of the degree of success being achieved.

Adam: This is very true: I think the most common thing said by people of my age is that they never get enough responsibility; also there is a lack of information on their performance and progress. I would have thought that what you have said about counselling in developing personal and social skills applied equally to developing technical skills?

Gaynor: Well yes, counselling should also play a part in this, but I can see that there are some differences. There seems to be quite a large body of knowledge about management techniques and acquiring this knowledge is comparatively easy. The application, however, is another matter. I am sure that we both know people who have accumulated numerous certificates to indicate that they have attended courses on everything from human relations to work study. In spite of this, they cannot use this knowledge. It may be that personal or social skills are lacking since these are inevitably part of implementing the technical knowledge.

Adam: You mean like devising a very efficient food and beverage control system which is deliberately sabotaged because of antagonistic management-staff relations?

Gaynor: Exactly. When thinking about how to carry out management development we can think of all these three skills. Management must involve them all simultaneously. You know, I only fully realised the real importance of this a short time ago. Years ago, when we started to expand as a company, I really was an amateur and when I think back to some of the things we did, it was quite appalling. But it is different today. We could take risks then because we were not very big but to learn by trial and error in a company of our size now would be to court disaster. So you see the importance to us in really getting to grips with management development.

Adam: There is one thing which we haven't really said anything about and that is wastage or turnover of managers. I can see that a pretty effective management development programme could be devised in terms of what each person is likely to do during the next

five years. This is particularly true of departmental heads in our
units and our trainees. But what sort of development can we provide
for those who are not unit managers? After all, we only have a small
number of people as head office staff even if a move to head office
was considered as a promotion.

Gaynor: If I may say so, this is another mistake that seems to be
made: confusing promotion with development. We should, I think,
continue to increase the salary of managers who develop and expand
their business. It would be a mistake to think that if they do this well
we should invent administrative positions to 'promote' them into.
Hotel managers can be given opportunity to develop by taking on
new assignments like moving to larger or different types of
operation. A manager of one of our city hotels with a highly
transient and mostly business customers might, for example, move
to an hotel on the coast. The relatively longer stay of customers
there may help develop his talents for entertaining people rather than
just providing accommodation.

Adam: In any case, we are bound to have some managers whose
full potential we cannot expect to exploit.

Gaynor: Yes, that is true. In any case I think that although we will
be sorry for them to leave the company, we must accept the
inevitability. In fact I would do as I have done before and do all that
I could to find the right sort of appointment with another firm. Too
many firms close their eyes to this and then express surprise when a
manager leaves.

Adam: I can see that different problems will arise in different firms.
With a relatively high turnover in managerial grades you can never
expect the counselling you advocate to work properly. It needs a
fairly stable staff for this to be introduced and for it to work. I
should imagine in this case all that a firm can do is rely on outside
courses to develop appropriate skills as well as they can.

Gaynor: So I should imagine. I would say that where this turnover
exists you can never have any management development. Perhaps
some management training, that's all. We train seals and dogs, so
you can see how I would rate such a firm!

Adam: So in talking about management development we are really
concerned with something that happens inside the firm and some
acquisition of techniques probably outside the firm. It seems rather
hard luck on the individual with potential whose firm does not have
the commitment or interest in his development.

Gaynor: For the younger man I wouldn't think it was too black a
picture. After all, he can keep changing jobs until he finds us! If he
has the right calibre though, I think he would try to offset difficulties
by reading and attending courses during his own time. I would

worry about how long he could continue do this as it would become very frustrating.

Adam: This reminds me of remarks made by participants at the end of some management courses, 'We agree with all that has been said, but really it is my boss who should be here—not me'. My response to this would be to point out that perhaps *their* subordinates say the same about them! We need to develop unit managers to appreciate that part of their role is to counsel their heads of departments and trainees. It would be inappropriate and impractical to put the onus for such counselling on our own head office staff. I have heard it said that it takes a good manager to develop a good manager and it takes a professional to train a professional one!

Gaynor: I am always amused at this word 'professionalism'. I wonder what a professional is? The church, the law, and the army used to be very antagonistic against any other groups who called themselves a profession.

Adam: And I suppose that the 'oldest profession' would contest their claim! You might accuse me of splitting hairs again, but I would distinguish between 'a profession' and 'a Professional'. A profession has all sorts of distinguishing characteristics. It has an agreed body of knowledge, it has a code of conduct for its members, it generally has some form of formal entry requirements, and so on. From this point of view I cannot see that management can be regarded as a profession. Perhaps, in time, a case could be made for hotel management as a profession by adopting these criteria and we seem to be very close to this in our professional Association. But I would find it very difficult to see a factory manager in the same light as an hotel manager.

Gaynor: Is the difference so great? After all they do similar things, they both have to achieve the enterprise goals through their staff, they have to plan, they have to make decisions. If you take the law for example, there are criminal lawyers and those who specialise in commercial law. The thing they have in common is the basic principles of jurisprudence although the actual content of their work may be vastly different. Surely managers are similar to this, whatever the field of commerce or industry in which they may be engaged?

Adam: In some respects I think this is true. There is a discernible body of knowledge, although incomplete, on which a manager can draw. But I would hesitate to call this a common body of knowledge. In the first place a manager's behaviour is influenced by the technology of the situation, whether he is involved in mass productions, say, or single jobs each of which is unique. He also seems to be influenced in the way he behaves by the rate of change in the work situation. Rapidly changing conditions require a loose organisation with a lot of initiative and only vaguely defined responsibilities. A situation in which little change occurs seems to require a more bureaucratic managerial style. Finally the individual manager influences, in a major way, the interpretation of the body of knowledge. In any situation his beliefs and attitudes, indeed his whole value system effects his conduct and behaviour as a manager.

Gaynor: Well, I suppose that is true, particularly your last point. If management can't be a profession, then how can managers be professional?

Adam: To say somebody is a professional relates to their competence; when we go to a doctor or a lawyer, we have to trust their competence and believe that they will act in accordance to some standards. The extent to which an hotel manager does this indicates his degree of professionalism. So I would say that the professional hotel manager must have a reasonable body of knowledge. This includes knowledge of the social phenomena of operating an hotel both from the customer's point of view and that of his staff. Then he needs to look ahead and plan and make things happen rather than be controlled by events. He needs to adapt his actions to meet these anticipated events and not react routinely to cues. As a professional his decisions must be more often right than wrong, otherwise he is either lacking in his body of knowledge or is unable to apply it. Generally speaking a manager will be paid whether a banquet he offers is a tremendous success or an absolute disaster. But I would expect a professional manager to have more successes than failures or even mediocre ones. Above all, I would say that a professional manager builds a climate at work in which all his employees grow as individuals.

Gaynor: You start to become impassioned, Adam! You would regard a manager deficient on any of these as less than professional?

Adam: Well, I would certainly say that he needs to undergo management development to become a professional.

Gaynor: Ah yes, now, here is my wife: you have met?

Adam: Yes indeed, good evening Mrs. Gaynor.

Mrs. Gaynor: Good evening Mr. Smith, am I disturbing you? You seem to be very involved in something.

Adam: Not at all, Mrs. Gaynor, in fact I hadn't realised the time and I am going to be late. Would you excuse me?

Gaynor: Certainly Adam, we would not wish to prevent you developing your social skills!

Adam: Goodnight Mr. Gaynor. Goodnight Mrs. Gaynor.